THE RIDDLE OF RACISM

The
Riddle of Racism

S. CARL HIRSCH

The Viking Press   *New York*

ACKNOWLEDGMENTS

For a perceptive reading of the manuscript and helpful suggestions, I owe thanks to Professor I. A. Newby, Department of History, University of Hawaii. Similarly, I would like to express my gratitude to Professor C. Eric Lincoln, Union Theological Seminary, and Professor James A. Rawley, Department of History, University of Nebraska, for their comments on the manuscript. All three are distinguished historians whose works have provided some of the materials for this book.

In addition, I would like to thank the following for reading the early version of the manuscript and making useful comments: Professor Walter Bateman, Department of Anthropology, Rochester State Junior College; Anthony Downs, consultant to the National Advisory Commission on Racial Disorders; and Carey McWilliams, editor of *The Nation* and author of several outstanding books on race relations in America. Also, I would like to acknowledge the helpful comments of Jacob W. Gruber, Professor of Anthropology and Director, Temple University, College of Liberal Arts in Rome; and Brad Byers, National Research Council, National Academy of Sciences.

Four young friends acted as a "readers' jury," offering helpful viewpoints: Todd Bannor, Jay Hall, and Robin and Mark Lewy. My junior-high class on racial discord at the Evanston Unitarian Church provided the sounding board for the main ideas in this book.

My special thanks go to my wife, Stina L. Hirsch, a supportive assistant in every sense. The Notes on Sources were largely her work.

For the Walls—
in hope of more days to share

Contents

THE RIDDLE OF RACISM

Notes on Sources, covering the factual material in this book, may be found beginning on page 203.

THE PROBLEM
"Are Ye Going to Resist?"

For thousands of years men have been aware that they differed in racial features. But here in America, for the first time anywhere at any time, the three great racial groupings of mankind came together on the same soil in large numbers.

To this land came Europeans, filled with a belief in their own natural superiority over all other peoples of the earth. They came as settlers, but also as warriors, prepared to wrest this land from its residents by force.

Here lived native populations. The Europeans labeled them Indians—through an error which was never corrected. The physical appearance of these natives seemed to link them to Asian backgrounds. They were classified as racially "different," and inferior.

Shackled and price-tagged, large numbers of black people were brought here by the Europeans. These were Africans, torn from their loved ones, their homelands, their freedom. The white captors turned them into slaves, personal property, hardly more than domesticated animals.

Under this set of conditions, the meeting of the three great races on America's soil was not likely to be a happy one.

And yet, this was also a land where men had come to share freedom. The hope for liberty in their hearts fed their courage to struggle and overcome great problems. In America they built the world's first modern government based on democracy.

So here then are the two parts of a paradox. Why did

the United States proclaim the equality of *all* men—and uphold the superiority of *some*?

Our history as a nation speaks to us in such riddles. A search for answers leads on two twisting paths. One course seeks to unravel the snarl of race turmoil that continues to trouble all America. The other quest traces the discovery of small bits of fact which together make up a modern understanding of "race."

Our story tells of people probing for truth—a collector of human skulls and a white man living among Indians; a remarkable runaway slave and a scientist compelled to turn against his homeland; the secret of a "living human fossil," who suddenly emerged from the wilderness; and a strange revelation by children playing with dolls.

Much of the evidence to be examined is not pretty or comforting. Involved here is the agony of America's black people, denied life, liberty, and the pursuit of happiness in a nation that promised it all to everyone.

The ordeal of this nation is shared by many white Americans, who became ridden with unreasoning hatred and a deep sense of guilt.

This is also the story of Abraham Lincoln, and of Thomas Jefferson before him. Their plight was this: they lived out their lives in a confused age in which they and their fellow Americans remained confounded by the mystery of human races.

Jefferson's "Suspicion"

Dozing, Thomas Jefferson came wide awake with the sound of the work bell. It was cold in the room, and dark except for the light of a single guttering candle.

As he twisted in his chair, the statesman groaned with pain running through his entire body. His head was a mass of bruises, and his bandaged leg lay propped high on pillows.

The faintest sunglow had just barely begun to light up this working day in the late spring of the year 1782. The big house on the hill was silent. Upstairs, the statesman's wife was dying after childbirth. In grief, Jefferson had wandered about the surrounding foothills on horseback—until a nasty fall had confined him with bruises and aches.

From his study window he could dimly see perhaps a hundred of his slaves going to work in the fields. He turned to the book he was writing and made a note about "the unhappy influence on the manners of our people produced by the existence of slavery among us."

Seven years before, in drafting the Declaration of Independence, Jefferson had used strong language in denouncing slavery. He described the slave system as "a cruel war against human nature," "an assemblage of horrors," and expressed outrage at "a market where *MEN* should be bought and sold." The South demanded that these words be stricken out. For the sake of colonial unity, Jefferson settled for the simple declaration that "all men are created equal"—a phrase that was to haunt the conscience of the new nation.

Jefferson was a slaveowner with a loathing for slavery. He had a strong personal distaste for all forms of tyranny and oppression. But while he wanted, and even tried, to bring about slavery's end, he did not give up his own slaves during his lifetime nor did he set them all free in his will.

Jefferson approached the problem as a dedicated student of natural science. However, the science of his time could offer little truth on the meaning of human races. In his book, *Notes on the State of Virginia*, Jefferson was putting together his own observations. He had a "suspicion," he wrote, that "the blacks . . . are inferior to the whites in the endowment both of mind and body."

It was just that—a suspicion based on nothing even vaguely resembling scientific study. "If some races were inferior to others . . ." then this might justify—what? The forbidding of citizenship to men of certain skin colors? The withholding of human rights? The barring of equal opportunities? The denial of a man's ownership of his own body and soul?

The problem lay like a teasing riddle in Jefferson's thought. Almost all white Americans were certain that they were members of a better race than were the slaves. They believed devoutly in their own racial supremacy as a law of nature, as a commandment of God. Jefferson was that rare white man of early America who puzzled over the truth.

Firebell in the Night

By the year 1791, Jefferson had become Secretary of State. He worked in cramped, temporary quarters in Philadelphia. That year his interest in science brought him a new and disquieting look at the black man.

The Virginian was now deep into endless problems which beset the young government. One big project was the nation's new capital now being planned in the wilderness area which was to become Washington, D.C. Jefferson had employed as a surveyor of the site a free Negro named Benjamin Banneker, a Maryland farmer with some astounding talents.

The Secretary of State was attracted to Banneker as a man whose interests were much like his own. An amateur inventor and scientist, Banneker had never had Jefferson's educational opportunities. And yet the black man had become an acknowledged master of higher mathematics and astronomy.

To the Secretary's desk in August 1791 came a bulky package from Benjamin Banneker, the manuscript of an almanac he had written—a book of scientific and practical value, containing much vital information. Amazed and delighted, Jefferson leafed through the calculations on the motions of heavenly bodies, tides, eclipses, the risings and settings of the sun, as well as weather predictions, the listing of tables, important public dates, and other useful facts.

Banneker's *Almanac* was to become a standard reference work, sold throughout America and the world, published annually in large editions. Jefferson was elated to receive an advance copy. He was less pleased with the letter that came with the manuscript.

"I am of the African race," the writer affirmed proudly. Banneker went on to say what troubled him—Jefferson's inconsistent record of public declarations and private deeds with regard to Negroes.

A quiet and modest man, Banneker addressed Jefferson with respect, and even admiration. He had heard of Jefferson's dislike of slavery. But he urged that the Virginian now throw off "that train of absurd and false ideas and opinions" which white men hold toward blacks.

This appeal went right to the core of the contradiction that pulled Jefferson in two opposing directions. Banneker urged that the great American patriot look back to the years when the struggle against British rule brought Jefferson into open conflict with those who held others in the grip of tyranny and injustice. "You were then impressed with the great violation of liberty," recalled Banneker.

How then can you, Jefferson, "be found guilty of that most criminal act which you professedly detested in others?" Banneker asked. How could you, the designer of American freedom, violate your own principles "in detaining by fraud and violence so numerous a part of my brethren, under groaning captivity and cruel oppression?"

The hard accusation stared at Jefferson from the handwritten page. Stunned and bewildered, the statesman spent the next ten days preparing a reply, the argument running on feverishly in his brain.

Could it be true that slavery was based on a false and unscientific view of the black race? Was it possible that Negroes *appeared* backward only because of "the imbecility of their present existence" as slaves? Could the black man rise to the level of the white man if given the opportunity? One answer seemed obvious from the intricate scientific data in Banneker's *Almanac*.

"Nobody wishes more than I do," Jefferson wrote to Banneker, "to see such proofs as you exhibit that nature has given to our black brethren talents equal to those of the other colors of men."

Jefferson's lame response satisfied no one—least of all himself. The Virginian lived out his long life finding no relief from the tormenting problem of race that seared his mind. Nearing eighty, Jefferson revealed to a friend, "This momentous question, like a firebell in the night, awakened and filled me with terror."

In spirit he rebelled against the slave system. But the "suspicion of Negro inferiority" undermined all of his efforts in fighting slavery. In the end he contented himself with a distant vision that "nothing is more certainly written in the book of fate than that these people are to be free."

However, it would be left to others to bring life to Jefferson's words. His promise of equality would kindle hope in each new generation. The cause of human freedom would burn fierce and defiant—as it did in the heart of a black youth named Frederick.

A Slave Fights Back

Long before the Monday morning work bell, the young slave forked down hay from the barn loft. Descending, he suddenly became aware of the master, Edward Covey, just below him.

Covey grabbed the boy's legs and the two went crashing to the barn floor. In the lantern's rays, Frederick glimpsed a fierce, evil smile.

"I've got ye now, black devil!" Covey snarled. In another instant he would have had a rope tied securely around the slave's legs.

Quickly Frederick twisted, leaped free. Covey charged the boy, ramming him against a post, pounding him with his huge fists. Desperate, Frederick threw his slender body against his attacker. He fastened his fingers on Covey's windpipe, his nails drawing blood. Choking, gagging, the slave master tore himself loose. In the darkness of the barn the two figures now crouched, lunged, circled.

In this year 1834, Covey was reputed up and down the Chesapeake shore as a slave-breaker. For owners with troublesome bondsmen, Covey was their man. He took on slaves like Frederick for a year, working them on his farm. They were left at Covey's mercy—and he had none.

Covey was hindered by only one condition. Slaves were valuable property and owners wanted them back alive— and preferably in one piece. Short of killing them, Covey agreed to crush out their pride, hope, and human dignity. He believed in sheer brute violence, in making the slaves feel the supremacy of the white man in their own bruised flesh.

The ambitious slave-breaker had just begun to build his personal fortune, hoping some day to own a string of slaves. But the threat to his future was there across from him that morning in the barn—the slave with ideas of liberty and of his own humanness!

The young black, Frederick, had been "spoiled" some years before by a former owner's soft-hearted wife, who began teaching the child to read. There the trouble began. White dogma of the day held that a Negro should know nothing but the will of his master and learn to obey it. A dozen states had strict laws against anyone who would teach a slave to read or write. "Learning will spcil the best slave in the world," was a saying in the South, fervently believed as gospel. For Covey there was no better proof than this defiant boy before him, suspected of aspiring to freedom!

Covey was a brawny monster stung now into savagery. "Are ye going to resist, you scoundrel?" the white man barked.

Frederick eyed his master with anger, but the words that came out of his mouth were polite, out of habit, "Yes, Sir."

Frederick had suffered months of Covey's brutal floggings. They had had their effect. At one time he became certain that he could stand no more. "I am, in fact, broken," he had told himself, shattered as he was in spirit and in his pain-racked body.

Then came this last week. New blows had opened old wounds. The pounding had crushed his battered bones. He lived through torture and terror, finally crawling off into the woods to hide and heal himself.

He lay there in agony hating the world, Covey, himself. The slave-breaker had hardly proved himself a member of a better race. To Frederick he was, in fact, a loathsome beast, without a trace of human decency. The boy despised him also as a breeder of slaves: Covey owned a young black woman, Caroline, bought at the slave market to be used like a farm animal for bearing children into slavery.

Frederick saw no chance of escape from this brute, no course except to face Covey's madness once again. He had returned on a Sunday, a day when the pious Covey prayed in church like a man without sin. Before sunup Monday, Covey came to the barn to find his errant slave and to teach him his place.

Neither the black slave nor the white master was prepared for the kind of encounter that was now going on in the barn. The nation's learned men, lawmakers, clergymen, scientists—all were agreed in advance as to who would be the superior person in such a contest. But clearly something was going wrong here. White supremacy was chiseled deeply into this nation's cornerstone. The doctrine held that every white man excelled every black man in every way. How could it be violated by a slim, black youth?

For an hour and more the two traded blows. Covey, in a cold fury, could not bring his prey to earth. The slave darted, kicked, writhed, deftly landed some smashing blows.

Frederick hardly knew himself. Yesterday the young slave had been a wrung-out rag of a human being, limp, docile, cowering. But now something strange had happened. Frederick felt a new courage welling within. Fear had fled from him. He might die defending himself, but no longer would he take the lash across his bare shoulders, the heel kick in his groin, the club drawing blood from a head wound.

The young slave was resolved to fight—and to win. Suddenly, he realized that the white man across from him no longer appeared supreme. The man's color no longer held him in terror!

"Are ye still going to resist?" Covey sobbed, unbelieving.

The blood gushed from his nose and from a cut across the eye.

"For six months you have treated me like a brute," Frederick replied calmly, forcefully, "but you have whipped me for the last time!" Lithe and quick, the boy repulsed every attack with slashing blows.

"Hughes!" Covey cried. "Hughes, help me!" His cousin came in the barn door and charged at Frederick. A quick kick in the belly sent Hughes running, not to return.

"Caroline!" screamed Covey, calling frantically for aid from the slaves who worked around the place. The blacks came by the open door, peered in, and went about their duties elsewhere.

Through Frederick's mind flashed the idea that he might be hanged for hitting a white man. Then he realized that Covey would not call in the authorities, as it would ruin his reputation as a slave-breaker to admit publicly what he had suffered at the hands of a half-grown boy.

Frederick could now see that the slave master was stealthily working his way toward a piece of fence rail near the barn door. But before Covey could snatch the wooden club, the young slave pitched him headlong into the barnyard.

A clouded, hazy dawn now spread through the eastern woods. In the half-light, Covey sprawled, bleeding and filthy, near the dung heap. The young victor stood weary, heaving, a sense of his own manhood surging through him. The battle of the barnyard was over.

The young slave was soon to be renowned as Frederick Douglass, fighter for freedom—for the very goal this entire country professed to hold dear.

"Troublesome Property"

By the 1840s, young America was a nation with a nightmare. Its goals in those years were an improved democracy, wider prosperity, and a country unified and expanding westward. A deep gulf lay between those who enjoyed the new surge of progress and those who did not. With every passing year, the gap widened.

It was a time when the new nation was trying to extend its liberty, introducing free public schools and libraries, easy access to newspapers, new forms of political action for the common man, the right to vote for those without property. At the same time, America tightened its iron grip on the vast black population.

A slave could not vote, own property, appeal to the courts, secure an education, or get married legally. Unable to protest, he was forced to accept any hardship or punishment at his master's whim. The rape of a woman slave by a white owner was not a crime. As a piece of property for his entire lifetime, a bondsman could be inherited, traded, sold. To these inhuman, unbending laws, the slave states added more severe ones constantly.

In the North, slavery had proved to be unworkable and unprofitable. It was abolished there at the urging of many of the nation's founders who could not square the ideals of the Revolution with the idea of slavery. Nevertheless, black freedmen remained hated outcasts, barred from northern white society, from skilled trades and schools, from polls and juries. They were denied citizenship and the simplest of constitutional rights in New England, in the very Cradle of Liberty.

The South soon began its successful fight for a strong fugitive-slave law in Congress. It was designed to turn all America into a nation of slave catchers.

Meanwhile, in the slave states, blacks resisted in a thousand ways. And yet, the South flourished as new machinery and new markets made cotton king. Blacks revolted, ran away by the thousands. And still, fabulous wealth was enjoyed by big slaveowners. Year by year, an economy resting squarely on the backs of unpaid Negro slaves yielded increasing riches.

The share which the slave drew from this growing prosperity was exactly nothing. In fact, the brutality became worse. The whips cracked. The rules became tighter. The southern slaveholder kept his bondsman in dire want, used up his body, and sent him early to the grave.

What did the planter expect from his slaves in return for all this misery, grief, and terror? A loyal and devoted willingness to serve, perhaps? A full sense of cooperation? An eagerness by the black man to offer every bit of his skill, diligence, and imagination?

To the best of his ability the slave tried to see that the master received his just due. Many a black bondsman became an expert at negligence, damage, and error. Often he was brilliant at frustrating his master's needs.

At harvest time he was seized with a sudden blindness, or his fingers became strangely paralyzed. Did the master's carriage break down? Then the slave ran and fetched a tool—the wrong one. Was he ordered to burn out a stump? Too bad—the fire ran wild and burned down the barn. Slaves were sent to the dock with a shipment of cotton— and somehow just missed the boat!

Exasperated, a North Carolina planter in the 1840s confessed in a letter to his kinfolk that slaves were "a troublesome property." Often a slave was eager to produce more chaos than crops. If he was "worthless" to his master, that was exactly what he intended to be. The slave knew that if he took great pains to improve the white man's land or to enrich his crop or fatten his hogs—he would not gain an ounce of food or a shred of freedom.

A sharp-eyed Massachusetts traveler jotted down what he saw in the South:

> A master cannot force his slave to reason, to remember, or, except in certain cases, to hear or see. If he is sent with a message, he forgets it. He never considers that if the fence is broken, the cattle will get among the corn; and if they do, he neither sees nor hears them. The thing he is commanded to do, that single thing he does, nothing else.

The northern observer further described the slave:

> He is set to planting corn. The seed, it chances, is worm-eaten and decayed. What is that to him? He goes on planting. It is just so in everything else. . . . Whatever capacity or understanding he may have, he sinks it, hides it, annihilates it, rather than its fruits should be filched from him by his owner.

One exasperated southern overlord complained of a field-hand, "Let a hundred men show him how to use a hoe or a wheelbarrow, he'll still grasp one by the bottom and the other by the wheel."

The cruel slave driver was sometimes driven to the point of madness. Many slaves were clever at *failing* to learn. Pushed hard under the whiplash, they "loafed" artfully whenever the overseer's back was turned. If the system robbed the slave of his labor and his freedom, he readily stole what he could in return. Often that was the way of survival.

Outwitted, the slaveholder constructed for himself a consoling fantasy. Clearly, he said, the black man was stupid and dishonest, childlike and lazy. There could be little doubt, the southern planter society concluded, that the African race was inferior and that its members were unable and unwilling to learn and needed the governing hand of the white man.

In conjuring up this myth, the plantation owner found some comfort. Slavery was a grim, brutal business—and the vexed slave master looked for ease of mind wherever he could find it. He turned to his clergyman for soothing words, for something to help justify the inhuman relationships that surrounded him.

The churchmen of the South unearthed a buried fable which they offered as a biblical explanation of black men and their origins. Negroes were the offspring of Ham, the sinful son of Noah, they said. And blackness was God's curse upon all of Ham's descendants. Somehow this story seemed to put the Lord's blessing on Negro slavery.

And yet, many a slaveowner was troubled. If he didn't sleep well, it was not only because he thought he heard the conspiring voices of black men in the night or feared he would soon be murdered in his bed. He searched the books of law, religion, philosophy by candlelight for a comforting word.

Perhaps science held the answer. The slaveowner appealed to the learned men for a doctrine to do double duty: to help keep black men in bondage and to free white men from their guilt!

THE EIGHTEEN FIFTIES
"A Decided Superiority"

The sound of metal striking bone echoed in the laboratory. Into the large container, Dr. Samuel G. Morton carefully poured the buckshot pellets. The container was a human skull.

Clearly this was a scientist at work. And as America moved into the mid-nineteeenth century, Dr. Morton was one of the most highly respected scholars in the nation. In his spacious Philadelphia laboratory, his life's work was on display.

Human skulls—a thousand of them. They were arrayed neatly in their cabinets, the sun glinting on their shiny domes. Classified, labeled, segregated, they were Dr. Morton's vision of mankind, divided into five distinct races.

To this collection, skulls had been shipped from all over America. A large number of them had been picked off bone piles on the western plains, the remains of slain Indians. Others had come from graveyards in the South where Negro slaves were buried. And still others were sent to Dr. Morton by missionaries, travelers, fellow scientists, from the far reaches of the world.

This was the finest collection of its kind anywhere, and Dr. Morton was proud. For years he had been engaged in the painstaking work of measuring his skulls in every possible manner. He filled them with buckshot and then poured it into a graduated cylinder to determine the capacity of each skull. He gauged the thickness of the bone, checked the length and breadth of each portion of the cranium, pondered the peculiarities of form and contour.

What he observed was set out in a massive book, splendidly illustrated. Dr. Morton was sure that he had discovered the key to the differences within mankind. In his neat arrangement of skulls, row upon row, he seemed to see the answer to the riddle of races.

Years before, while studying in Europe, he had visited a collection of skulls in Germany. The collector had one specimen that he prized above all others. It was the skull of a woman who had lived in the Caucasus, a mountainous area of southeastern Europe. Admired as a "perfect" specimen, this cranium brought rapturous praise from collectors everywhere. It was this Caucasian skull which became the inspiration for the term "the Caucasian race," meaning the white race.

In Dr. Morton's collection, the Caucasian skulls held the high place of honor. He seemed to see in them certain qualities without equal. He had no hesitation in describing the entire white race as "distinguished." In his book he declared, "This race attains the highest intellectual endowments."

Next came "the Mongolian race." Dr. Morton wrote: "In their intellectual character the Mongolians are ingenious, imitative and highly susceptible of cultivation." He then listed what he called "the Malay race" as "active and ingenious," with the habits of a migratory people who invade and prey on others.

"The American race" was Dr. Morton's name for the American Indians. He described his large number of Indian skulls, adding that this race is "averse to cultivation, and slow in acquiring knowledge; restless, vengeful, and fond of war, and wholly destitute of maritime adventure."

The bottom rank was assigned by the eminent Dr. Morton to "the Ethiopian race," people of African origins. In this race, he said, is to be found "the lowest grade of humanity."

There was some mystery about how Dr. Morton had arrived at all these conclusions. His research, he hinted, had something to do with the shape of skulls and even more with their size, suggesting that what was most important was the bulk of the brain. In these comparisons, he said, the white race had "a decided and unquestionable superiority over the nations of the earth."

Somehow, there was no white scientist who questioned his conclusions. In fact, Dr. Morton was held to be a foremost authority on the subject of race, an outstanding figure in the American scientific community.

He carried on a lively interchange with other reputed experts in the field. One of these was Dr. Josiah Clark Nott, a physician of Mobile, Alabama, who was to be hailed as one of the founders of the "American School of Anthropology."

Dr. Nott agreed with Dr. Morton wholeheartedly—and went a little farther. Dr. Nott considered the mentality of the black man to be "defective."

As a lecturer in his native South, Dr. Nott was very popular. He attracted a wide following in the plantation society and spoke a language that slaveowners enjoyed hearing. Superior and inferior races, said the anthropologist, "could not live together on any other terms than that of master and slave."

Using scientific terms, Dr. Nott said that the black man was hardly more than an animal, referring to various species of apes. The "pure-blooded Negro" was not capable of taking the first step toward civilization, added Dr. Nott, and no challenging voice was raised against him. As for American Indians, "It is in vain to talk of civilizing them," declared the learned southern doctor. "You might as well attempt to change the nature of a buffalo."

The Doctors Morton and Nott wrote letters back and forth between the North and the South. They were groping now, reaching, grasping for something new—an idea so bold that neither of them dared as yet to voice it in public.

Among the races, they seemed to see clear, marked, fixed differences. Could it be, they ventured, that men were not only of distinct races, but actually of different species? Perhaps white men and black men were really as different as dogs and cats.

Nott tried out the idea on some of his southern friends— and found they were interested. If such a notion could be proven, it would clearly show that there was nothing immoral or sinful in keeping "an inferior species" enslaved. The theory would add a powerful argument for keeping black and white separated.

As to the fact that black and white people could and did mate with one another, Dr. Nott had a ready explanation and dire warnings about that. His idea was contained in "mulatto," a degrading term taken from the word "mule" and referring to persons of mixed parentage. From the mating of a horse and a donkey, Dr. Nott pointed out, the resulting mule was sterile and could produce no offspring of its own. There were instances in biology where individuals of different species could mate, he warned, but the offspring was in some way deficient.

There was one hitch in the new theory of distinct species. It seemed to collide head-on with the Bible. The Old Testament clearly described all men as having a common parentage in the Garden of Eden. And neither Dr. Morton nor Dr. Nott felt they had enough authority to refute the Scriptures. Their hope lay in enlisting a man who was world famous in the field of natural science.

Harvard University had succeeded in bringing Louis Agassiz to its faculty in 1846. And what a prize catch he was! In Europe, Agassiz had been a big fish in a very large scientific sea. America was a small pond, just beginning to develop its own centers of scholarship and research. And Agassiz glided brilliantly into a dominant position in American science.

The Swiss-born Agassiz had never in his life seen a Negro before he came to this country. In Philadelphia he sat in a restaurant staring fixedly at the black men who were serving him. The following year Agassiz toured the South, and was an honored guest in the slave states. He was royally treated in Charleston, South Carolina, well paid for his lectures, with rich gifts added. One day he toured a large plantation, observing the slaves at work. And on the veranda of the great mansion he pondered the queries of his hosts as to the mystery of race and its meaning.

That evening Agassiz spoke to a glittering audience at the exclusive Literary Club of Charleston. Weighing his words carefully, the scientist offered his opinion that the various races came from distinct biological origins. A murmur of surprise ran through the assemblage as Agassiz added that Negroes and whites were "quite probably" members of separate species.

Agassiz's "expert" opinions were not missed by Dr. Nott. The Alabaman rubbed his hands in glee at each new pronouncement of the eminent scientist. Would Professor Agassiz lend his great weight to the effort to oust the Negro from the human race?

"With Agassiz in the war," read Dr. Nott's joyous message to Dr. Morton, "the battle is ours."

A Matter of Time

In their Sunday best, Americans of 1850 filed silently into houses of worship in cities and hamlets, and at country crossroads. This was a people steeped in the Scriptures.

Few had any doubts that the biblical stories were truth, word for word. They accepted the account of the earth's creation as set out in the Book of Genesis. Believing in Adam and Eve as earnestly as they did in their own grandparents, these God-fearing families were confident about their origins. If scholars had not yet found the exact geographical location of the Garden of Eden, they had clearly fixed the date of Adam's birthday.

Out of centuries of patient research by biblical probers, a respected clerical authority, the British Archbishop Ussher, presented a precise summary. The Creation had begun, he said, on October 23, in the year 4004 B.C. It was on the following Saturday that Adam was born.

With this information as a starting point, the renowned scientists Morton, Agassiz, and Nott raised a troublesome question. The official church version of man's time on earth was less than six thousand years. Was it possible that the racial varieties of mankind could have developed in so short a time?

If Adam and Eve were white, could so many of their descendants have become red, black, brown, and yellow in such a brief interval? And could they have scattered so quickly to the corners of the earth and there built their own cultures and societies?

No, said the experts. It could not possibly happen in six thousand years. It was well known, too, that the different races already existed at the time of Jesus Christ—which reduced the period for racial differentiation by almost two thousand years. Moreover, men of various races were clearly pictured on the ancient Egyptian tombs and monuments—thus reducing the time scale by an additional two thousand years.

To this riddle the scientists offered a solution of their own. Manlike beings, they said, were possibly created not once but several times, and in different places. True, the Bible failed to mention these incidents. But a Mongoloid "Adam and Eve" might have been formed somewhere in Asia. A black first couple might have appeared in Africa. And perhaps several other separate creations could have taken place in other parts of the world.

With the full weight of scholarly authority behind him, Professor Louis Agassiz stated that it was wrong to ascribe "to all living beings upon earth one common center of origin." His view opposed the biblical idea of a brotherhood of man.

Agassiz insisted that human beings had originated in more than one place, that there had been at least a dozen separate creations. This reasoning opened the possibility that members of other races were not fully human at all!

The scientists of 1850 seemed to be offering a doctrine that many white Americans yearned to believe. If Negroes did not belong to the human species, what was wrong with using them in the same way that men used any other domesticated beasts? Why should they not be owned, worked, traded as were livestock? And how could one speak of Negroes as being "created equal" with white people or sharing the rights of citizens?

Tempting as these ideas might be, especially in the slave states, they failed to win public approval. Somehow these notions clashed too violently with a religious tradition older than American slavery.

It was common for public speakers in the nineteenth

century to observe proudly that they were living in an "age of science." But in any open conflict between the word of scientists and that of the Holy Writ, most Americans clung firmly to their Bibles.

In the South, a stronghold of traditional religion, the theory of numerous acts of creation was firmly rejected. If the plantation society had to find a justification for slavery, this one would not do. A leading Virginia newspaper, the *Richmond Enquirer,* declared that the new doctrine of the scientists might be accepted by many of its readers as an excellent defense of slavery, but they would be wrong. The South could not approve such opinions if doubt in the Bible was to be "the price it must pay for them."

Running into such opposition, the esteemed scientists had the good sense to back off. They concentrated instead on an aspect of their race theory that was much more widely acceptable.

Teaching at Harvard, with nearby Boston one of the main centers of the growing antislavery movement, Agassiz cautiously avoided any views that might make him appear as a supporter of slavery. He emphasized a "safe" theory that had already been accepted in virtually all of white America.

Harvard's giant of learning tossed his leonine head and declared, "The very fact that races exist presses upon us the obligation to settle their relative rank." The races were unequal, Agassiz stated flatly, and the black race was "inferior." The one fatal argument to this theory was the black man himself.

Pretenders of Science

"Morton, Agassiz, Nott." The names were pronounced with contempt by the speaker on the platform.

"I say it is strange," cried Frederick Douglass, his voice ringing like a golden horn, "that there should arise such a phalanx of learned men—speaking in the name of *science*."

In his own years, Douglass recounted, a world shrunk by swift travel and the rapid spread of ideas had brought closer together the far-flung varieties of mankind. It was then odd indeed that a group of men, famed as scientists, should "forbid the magnificent reunion of mankind in one brotherhood."

The large audience at Western Reserve College sat hushed and tense as the speaker paused for breath. This was the school's graduation ceremony. The main speaker brought to the Cleveland campus on this occasion was a runaway slave named Frederick, who had taken the name Douglass after his escape to the North.

Douglass had come a long way in the twenty years since he had discovered his own manhood in that fierce barnyard encounter. He had fled from slavery, committing every ounce of his strength and every shred of his ability to the freeing of his fellow men.

As a fearless leader in the abolitionist movement, he was one of the most effective—a passionate and fluent speaker, a writer of prose that rang like steel on steel. He was editor of his own antislavery newspaper, a tireless worker in liberty's cause.

Now in his mid-thirties, he was a tall, proud-eyed man of purpose. On this warm evening in July 1854 he was ready as ever to do battle with the enemies of human freedom— even, he told his audience, against "the pretenders of science."

Step by step, Douglass led his listeners to the evidence that all races belong to the same human family. "Human rights stand upon a common basis," he said, clasping his outstretched hands. "All mankind has the same wants, arising out of a common nature."

Douglass took on the "scientific" theory that man sprang from several origins. Yes, he said, men do vary in form, feature, and color, but in nature there is nothing which points to "a new creation for every new variety."

In anger, the former slave showed that behind this false doctrine were sinister purposes. "You make plausible a demand for classes, grades and conditions," he charged, "and a chance is left for slavery, as a necessary institution."

Lashing at Morton, Agassiz, and Nott as men who "reason from prejudice rather than facts," he accused them of serving the slaveowner by "reading the Negro out of the human family."

Their theories were not harmless or academic ideas confined to the scientific laboratory or the college campus, said the black leader. He went on to show how these false doctrines were used that year in the debates in Congress in the effort to extend slavery into the western territories of the United States. "There is no doubt," added Douglass, "that Messrs. Nott, Morton and Agassiz were consulted by our slavery-propagating statesmen."

If the nation's leading scientists could produce only a twisted theory of mankind, Douglass declared sadly, then there was still some gap in America between "human love and human learning."

The echoes of applause had hardly died away when Douglass left that night, hurrying toward his next mission. He was far from happy in spite of the clear success of his speaking tour. The deeper problems of race, he feared, had hardly been touched on in this country. And even victory over slavery would not end the madness of prejudice raging in this land. Underlying the oppression of his people was white supremacy, the stubborn belief by America's white people that they were born into a master race.

Would the black man ever be acknowledged as an equal in America, a citizen with full rights, a fellow man with the full range of human gifts and needs? Douglass's own experiences as a black free man often left him with doubts and discouragement.

Slave or free, blacks were still looked upon by white America as being something less than human. And to Douglass's dismay, he had found that these same attitudes prevailed even among "the best friends of the black man," the white abolitionists.

For years he had worked alongside these liberal people who earnestly sought an end to slavery. He had seen them stoned and horsewhipped. In Illinois, an antislavery editor had been shot at his press. In Boston, a mob dragged an abolitionist leader through the streets with a rope around his neck. In several towns the headquarters of the Anti-Slavery Society had been burned to the ground. Still these brave and committed fighters carried on.

Most of them viewed slavery as immoral. And they carried on with religious fervor a crusade against what they saw as the most sinful institution in America. All across the nation that year of 1854, people were reading Harriet Beecher Stowe's heart-wringing story, *Uncle Tom's Cabin*. It brought thousands of people, stirred by the cruelty of the slave system, into the antislavery movement.

Every fresh advance won by the abolitionists brought closer the end of what Douglass called "the bludgeon and bloodhound civilization of the South." But he soberly took account of the shortcomings of most of the white abolitionists.

While Douglass urged the federal government to use

all possible means to destroy the slave system, the Anti-Slavery Society stood only for peaceful debate and moral persuasion. Whereas Douglass looked beyond abolition to the winning of full citizenship for blacks, the Society did not. Douglass urged that Negroes be permitted to work in the abolitionist movement. But the leaders saw only a limited role for the black man in winning his own freedom. In fact, Douglass felt himself hampered by the restrictions they tried to impose upon him as a leading orator and editor.

At the core of these weaknesses Douglass saw clearly the doctrine of white supremacy. While these friends were eager to fight against slavery, few were able to accept the slave's humanness. Although they condemned the slave-owner, they shared his fundamental belief in the everlasting mastery of the white race. Even among these devoted foes of slavery ran the unshaken belief that the black man was an inferior being, made so by nature.

Frederick Douglass had heard his people degraded by the most respected scientists in America, by the most revered religious leaders, by the nation's foremost lawmakers. The question of race was at that moment grinding its way slowly toward an opinion by the United States Supreme Court.

The Court Speaks

The date was March 6, 1857. In the musty basement courtroom, the thin voice of the aged man could barely be heard, and his fingers trembled as he turned the pages. For two hours he mumbled on.

Long-faced and owl-eyed Roger B. Taney, Chief Justice of the United States Supreme Court, read his decision against Dred Scott. The Missouri slave was fighting to be free. He had begun his legal battle twelve years before in St. Louis with two Negro attorneys. They could not get even a first hearing for him in the courts.

In time, Scott's case came to the attention of white abolitionists, and the slave himself came into the possession of owners who no longer believed in slavery. It was under these conditions that *Dred Scott* v. *Sandford* found its way into the nation's highest court as a test case. By now it not only involved one man's freedom but also wrapped up the most explosive issues of the pre-Civil War era.

Scott's troubled life as a slave was not an unusual one. Sold and resold, he had escaped once, only to be recaptured. He became the property of a Missouri army surgeon who was transferred to Illinois and later into the territory that was to become the state of Minnesota. Thus, for four years Scott lived with his master in the North as his personal servant.

Before returning to Missouri, Dred Scott remarried, and his wife gave birth to a daughter. He had lost his previous wife through a disaster common to slaves—she had been "sold away" to another owner.

In 1846, after his master had died, Dred Scott brought suit in St. Louis to have himself declared a free man. He claimed that he had lived for years on free soil, in a part of the country where slavery was prohibited by law—and that therefore he had ceased legally to be a slave.

By a vote of six to two, the United States Supreme Court said no to Dred Scott, adding that he was not a citizen, that as a slave he could not sue anybody in court for any reason, that he was the property of his owner who could not be unduly deprived of his property. The decision also threw into turmoil the political truce over the extension of slavery into new territories and toppled the tense power balance between North and South.

There was a long section of the *Dred Scott* decision, however, that hardly seemed to stir controversy in white America. In the name of the highest court of the land, Taney proclaimed the black man, enslaved or free, an inferior being who could never be regarded as a citizen. The Chief Justice said that the Negro was in permanent trouble in America not merely because he was a slave, but because he was black.

The equality of all men, proclaimed in the most sacred documents of this nation, "would seem to embrace the entire human family," observed Taney. "It is too clear for dispute that the enslaved African race were not intended to be included."

The Chief Justice recorded that in this land Negroes had always been regarded as "beings of an inferior order, and altogether unfit to associate with the white race, either socially or politically; and so far inferior that they had no rights which the white man was bound to respect." This opinion, he added, was fixed and universal among white people and "not open to dispute."

Sections of the *Dred Scott* decision became a burning issue in the elections of the following year. In Illinois, the two opposing candidates fought vigorously on most things in Taney's ruling. But on some things they were in agreement.

Lincoln Takes a Stand

Among the thirty-two states in the Union, river-bounded Illinois was probably the most divided, torn, and confused of all. The state was split across the middle on the issue of slavery.

To the town of Charleston, midway between the pro- and antislavery halves of Illinois, came two men in 1858 to debate their differences. One was "The Little Giant," Senator Stephen A. Douglas, squat and broad, a powerful voice in the capital at Washington and in the Democratic Party. Opposing him was a former congressman, the lanky country lawyer, Honest Abe Lincoln, candidate of the newly formed Republican party.

It was a hot mid-September day. Autumn was truly in the air—in haze, powdery road dust, and weed pollen. In the Charleston fairgrounds, farm families were showing off the best of their heifers and the plumpest of their pies.

Each political party blew its own trumpets, flaunted its colors, put on a show of glitter, noise, fireworks. The symbolic number of the day was thirty-two, Minnesota having just been admitted to the Union as the thirty-second state. A blaring brass band consisted of thirty-two couples, all on horseback. A bevy of thirty-two local girls paraded by, white-gowned and wreathed in prairie flowers. Toward afternoon, the large crowd, hot and fatigued, settled under the shade trees, waiting for the speeches to begin.

All of America was listening as well. This campaign for United States senator was confined to Illinois. But the contest matched two of the country's leading spokesmen on opposite sides of the most controversial issues in a nation facing civil war.

Each of the two candidates, Lincoln and Douglas, had spent the early summer zigzagging across the state, both drawing large crowds. In August Lincoln had challenged Douglas to face-to-face encounters. Then followed a series of debates from the same platforms. The rivalry turned raw and bitter.

A dozen issues were being debated. But at the heart of the conflict was the issue of slavery, the right and wrong of it. Should slavery be ended or continued, extended or limited? Should the nation halt the agony of living "half-slave and half-free," or should the South be permitted to go its own proslavery way in order to preserve the Union?

In Ottawa, Illinois, Douglas taunted Lincoln as favoring not only freedom for Negroes but also full equality. As for himself, Douglas confidently exclaimed:

> I believe this government was made by white men, for the benefit of white men and their posterity forever.
>
> I am in favor of confining citizenship to white men, men of European birth and descent, instead of conferring it upon Negroes, Indians and other inferior races.

At each debate, the two statesmen wrangled for three hours or more. Lincoln appeared as plain and homegrown as a warty squash, and yet with some deep-running power that made men edge closer as he spoke.

Douglas was skilled in spell-casting, a master at mockery, scorn, and ridicule. The senator drew for his white listeners a graphic picture of the problems in ending slavery, the freeing of four million blacks, the riotous and confusing aftermath. Would the former slaves become voters, citizens, on a par with white men?

In Jonesboro, Illinois, Senator Douglas again jeered at his opponent and charged that Lincoln believed that the Declaration of Independence included Negroes in the statement that "all men are created equal."

"In my opinion, the signers of the Declaration had no reference to the Negro whatever," Douglas shouted, waving a clenched fist in Lincoln's direction. "They desired to express by that phrase white men, men of European birth and European descent."

The arrival of the debate caravan in Charleston, Illinois, was for Lincoln a return to his own boyhood countryside, the scenes of the prairie lawyer's youthful years.

Just before noon, Lincoln answered a knock on his hotel

room door. The elderly white man who came to see him had known Lincoln as a boy, remembered his folks. There was a plea in the old man's face and tears in his eyes. Did Lincoln really believe that Negroes were the equal of white people?

That morning, Lincoln came face-to-face with his own personal beliefs and with the conflict in the nation. For twenty years he had spoken out vigorously against slavery. But the question he confronted this day was a deeper one. White men in America might differ on slavery for a variety of moral or practical reasons of their own. And here Lincoln thought about the crowd outside waiting to hear the debate. Was there a single voter among them, proslavery or antislavery, who regarded the Negro as his equal? Not likely.

Lincoln was running on the ticket of a new political party —but this too would be a party of, by, and for white men, and its candidates would be the same.

It was shortly before three o'clock when Abraham Lincoln rose to his towering height, beginning the Charleston debate. Lincoln said quietly that he would devote five minutes to discuss the equality of races. Instantly, silence spread out in a wave to the farthest edge of the crowd.

"I am not nor ever have been in favor of bringing about in any way the social and political equality of the white and black races," the Republican candidate said soberly. Scattered applause broke out, and a few muffled cheers.

"There is a physical difference between the white and black races which I believe will forever forbid the two races living together on terms of social and political equality," Lincoln declared, weighing each word.

"While they do remain together there must be the position of superior and inferior," he went on, "and I, as much as any other man, am in favor of having the superior position assigned to the white race." The hushed crowd released its tension with an outbreak of vigorous applause and lusty cheering.

Lincoln would lose the election for the senate that year. But two years later, he was to defeat Douglas in the contest for president of the United States. He would, in the years ahead, undergo the agonies of a man trying to square his own humanitarian beliefs with the political needs of the nation.

He was not an abolitionist. And yet no one had spoken out more forcefully than he about the moral evil of slavery. A staunch foe of the bigotry of his day, Lincoln was sincerely disturbed by the bondage of black people. But as the nation moved toward Civil War, neither Lincoln nor any other white leader in America had challenged the myth of the master race. For the time being, the dogma of white supremacy remained intact.

The war of words crackling on the Illinois prairie would soon give way to deadly gunfire at Antietam and Shiloh, Chickamauga and Gettysburg. And the issue of slavery would one day be settled. But the conflict over race was to rage on—for a hundred years, and more.

In the closing days of the 1850s, longshoremen on the New York City docks unloaded a wooden crate from a British freighter. Enclosed were copies of a small book, newly printed and green-bound. The book would figure importantly in the running controversy over man, his beginnings, his varieties.

The British biologist, Charles Darwin, had written his explosive account of the *Origin of Species*. To those involved in America's stormy debate, the subtitle of the book was most intriguing. It read: *The Survival of Favored Races in the Struggle for Life*.

THE CIVIL WAR YEARS
"What Will We Do with Them?"

New Year's day, 1860. A decade of raging strife was beginning with strange stillness. Tension hung everywhere in a brittle layer—like the crusted snow of a frigid New England night.

The anxious feeling was there at the fireside of Asa Gray, where a circle of learned men had gathered for sherry and talk. It was science talk mainly, with all eyes on the Harvard botanist and the small green book in his hand.

"Listen to this." Asa Gray read Darwin's words of hope in *Origin of Species*—that from its pages, "light will be thrown on the origin of man and his history."

Light of any kind was sorely needed. All of America cowered that winter in the dark fear of war. Rivalries between North and South were a murky tangle of opposing interests, goals, beliefs. Within a knotted snarl of hatreds lay unsolved riddles of race, bound up in the issue of slavery.

In the Capitol in Washington, D. C., southern congressmen were whispering treason in secret gatherings, pledging their states to unity, to secession and war if need be.

John Brown was less than a month in his grave. The fiery abolitionist had capped a lifetime of antislavery work with a daring raid on the federal arsenal at Harper's Ferry, Virginia. After Brown was captured and hanged, the New England naturalist Henry David Thoreau remarked that he, in death, seemed "more alive than he ever was."

Abraham Lincoln was just then driving his one-horse buggy across the storm-dark Kansas prairie. To small clusters of homesteaders, he spoke of slavery and war and his main hope of preserving the Union. Lincoln was cam-

paigning quietly for the presidency of the United States—
without being sure he really wanted it.

On the campus of Harvard University, the issue of slavery
and the problems of science were somehow joined in one.
Slavery in America had long been justified on the pseudo-
scientific grounds that black men were inferior; that black
and white people were "probably" members of different
biological species, with separate origins.

What if the theory could be proven false? The noted
botanist, Asa Gray, was struck with the power of Darwin's
ideas. He was not certain that the British biologist was
entirely correct. Nor did Gray suppose that the violent rivalries now clashing in America might be suddenly halted by
the appearance of a new scientific theory.

But Gray could not help wondering how Darwin's book
would be greeted by those scientists who had become
America's experts on the subject of race. The top authority
was a man whom he saw daily on the Harvard campus—
Louis Agassiz. Gray and his scholarly friends who had read
Origin of Species had come to one sober conclusion: If
Darwin was right, then Agassiz was wrong.

As for Agassiz, he could hardly wait to finish reading
Origin of Species before he offered his judgment. "A mis-
take," Agassiz fumed. "Untrue, unscientific, mischievous!"
In the South, Dr. Josiah Nott echoed his opinion about
Darwin, "The man is crazy."

Asa Gray sprang quickly to the defense of the British
biologist. Gray and Agassiz had tangled before on scientific
matters. Now the two Harvard scientists became locked
in a bitter dispute that divided the academic and scientific
worlds in halves. Agassiz and Gray battled on the lecture
platforms and in the pages of the learned journals. In the
months that followed, Gray became the chief spokesman
for Darwin's ideas in America.

In his own right, Gray was a scientist of top rank. The tall, kindly Yankee botanist had gathered more information than any other man on America's plant life. His view of nature tallied closely with that of Darwin. He had observed how "favored races" of plants were selected by nature, their successful traits being passed down from one generation to the next. As Darwin explained, such favored races were those which had adapted well to their surroundings, thereby increasing their chances for survival. Far from being fixed in place forever, races in all of nature were subject to change.

For many years Gray had been a close friend of the British biologist. In letters that went back and forth across the ocean they shared their strong interest in botany. They chatted about the special life styles of primroses and orchids and cowslips. Darwin was then deep in the twenty-year study that would lead to his theory of the evolution of plant and animal species.

As his search drew him closer to an answer that would overturn the traditional views of life on earth, Darwin grew more concerned. His findings showed that living forms had not been originally created as they now existed. Instead, they had evolved slowly across millions of years from a common ancestry. In a letter, the brooding, full-bearded Englishman wrote, "It is like confessing murder."

As for applying his theories to mankind, Darwin frankly backed away from the task, for the time being. He wanted to "avoid the whole subject so surrounded with prejudices," he said, "though I fully admit it is the highest and most interesting problem."

But an America in the throes of dispute over race and slavery could not evade the human questions. Darwin's book indicated clearly that man had been on the earth for a much longer time than anyone had believed. And Gray was quick to point out that Darwin had destroyed "the strongest argument for the plurality of human species."

Darwin's book had already achieved "one good effect," argued Gray. It showed "the races of men to be one *species,* that they are of one *origin.*"

As one species, mankind had lived on this earth through what Gray called "the long vista of the past." In the time scale of countless generations, the botanist declared, "the first step backward makes the Negro and the Hottentot our blood-relations."

Fossil Facts

Asa Gray was not altogether satisfied with *Origin of Species.* In some respects, the book clashed with his own deeply religious views. For Gray, there were at least two missing pieces needed to complete the unity of Darwin's theory. One of these was the explanation of how living things acquired and passed on new traits.

At that very moment, the first steps in answering that problem were being taken in another part of the world. Gregor Mendel, an Augustinian monk, was experimenting with honeybees, mice, and pea plants. His work was hardly known beyond his village, located in a remote part of what was then Austria. The monk had discovered the patterns by which certain characteristics reappear in successive generations of living things.

Mendel's theory would begin to explain some important truths about mankind's races. But the work of the science-minded monk was to lie buried in obscurity for another forty years.

In still other parts of Europe men were digging at bits and pieces of the remaining problem that troubled Asa Gray. If Darwin was correct, and man had been present on the planet for perhaps hundreds of thousands of years, then the earth must hold some clues to his former existence. Asa Gray watched carefully the scientific siftings of gravel from quarries, riverbeds, and caves.

Stone tools, burial ornaments, and ancient bones were objects of study far removed from Gray's primary interest in plant life. But with the publication of *Origin of Species,* the botanist suddenly found himself fascinated by the deeper questions of human origins.

By the year 1860, very few fossils of early man had been found. But Gray was strongly impressed "with the discovery in Europe of remains and implements of prehistoric races of men."

In March of that year came news of an important find in the Picardy region of France. "In plain language," Gray explained in an article linking these discoveries with Darwin's theory,

> these workers in flint lived in the time of the mammoth, of a rhinoceros now extinct, and along with horses and cattle unlike any now existing.
>
> Their connection with existing human races may perhaps be traced through the intervening people of the stone age, who were succeeded by the people of the bronze age, and these by workers in iron.

Did mankind appear in the ancient ages as varied in size, shape, and color? And did one race survive—to become the parent race of all existing peoples, of all races? The scientific curiosity of Asa Gray ran out to where darkness veiled the human past. Nor could the rising tumult of the living present be shut out.

Suddenly, events began to swirl violently in the botanist's contemporary world. Lincoln was elected president that autumn. The Illinois Republican took the oath of office on a damp, blustery day the following March. Forty days later,

Confederate cannon roared at Fort Sumter, South Carolina —and the Civil War was on.

Asa Gray, now in his fifties, threw himself heart and soul into the Yankee cause. He joined zealously in a company of militia guarding the arsenal near Harvard. Botany was all but forgotten in the excitement of the times. Darwin in Britain sided wholeheartedly with the North. And Gray kept him posted on the battle news in a series of letters signed, "Your cordial friend and true Yankee . . ."

"The South is now doomed," gloated the botanist after one northern victory. "Ill usage of Negroes will soon be unheard of."

To another friend he wrote, "I am no *abolitionist,* but if the rebels and scoundrels persevere, I go for carrying the war so far as to liberate every Negro." Gray added one disturbed afterthought, "Tho' what we are to do with this population, I see not."

A Leader Falters

Asa Gray was not alone. On the Union side of the Civil War, the same question was heard constantly. "What will we do with the black slaves—grant them freedom, citizenship, equality?" White America shuddered at the thought.

President Lincoln carefully weighed the military advantages of freeing the slaves and bringing them fully into the war against the South—at the risk of antagonizing slaveholders in the Border States who had remained neutral in the war.

The President wavered, stalled. His silence was that of a man in a quandary. Late nights in the White House, Lincoln mulled alone the problems that had baffled leaders of the nation since its founding days. He was torn between the prevailing white supremacy beliefs of his time and his private dreams of human brotherhood and democracy.

The South had no such confusion about its own attitudes on race. The vice-president of the Confederacy, Alexander Stephens, made it clear, "Our new government rests upon the great truth that the Negro is not equal to the white man; that slavery, subordination to the superior race, is his natural and normal condition."

The wartime Congress in Washington, D. C., representing Union opinion, didn't argue the matter. With hardly a dissenting voice, both houses declared that "this war is not waged upon our part. . . for any purpose of overthrowing or interfering with the rights or established institutions of . . . southern States."

A year of bitter warfare flowed by in blood. Much of the Union Army was encamped deep in slave territory—but no government announcement declared that this was now free soil. Thousands of blacks escaped from the South through the Union lines, and no one offered them liberty. Four million slaves heard no assurance from the Union government that they would ever be free.

The tight-lipped man in the White House, who had so often spoken out bitterly against slavery, said nothing. Hardly a day went by that black leaders, or white abolitionists, did not demand that he act. However, Lincoln was well aware that a majority of white Americans did not favor the abolition of slavery.

The President received a thousand callers, some carrying long petitions, urging that he issue a proclamation of freedom. At protest meetings in a hundred towns, antislavery societies cried out for emancipation of the slaves. An abolitionist leader charged that the Lincoln leadership was "stumbling, halting, weak." Frederick Douglass pointed out that "to fight against slaveholders, without fighting against slavery, is but a half-hearted business, and paralyzes the hands engaged in it."

The late summer of 1862 found the Union armies in a desperate defense of the nation's capital. Outnumbered Confederate armies were somehow winning stunning victories. Federal forces were hampered by poor support, low morale, and even the possibility of traitors within the high command.

As if the military problems were not enough, Lincoln was faced with knotty policy questions which defied clear answers. By August the President had decided how he would deal with the race problem. Like a military commander, he decided to move at once on three fronts. Which would be the real thrust and which the feints? He hardly knew himself.

Three Moves

Just after a brief lunch, the President walked into a conference room where a small group of black men was waiting for him. For all of his back-country upbringing, Lincoln was a skilled politician, with all the winning arts of handling people. He made his guests feel reasonably comfortable, and then began a strange prepared speech.

"You and we are different races," said the President. "I think your race suffer very greatly, many of them by living among us, while ours suffer from your presence."

To the silent men sitting before him, Lincoln went on to explain that even when Negroes cease to be slaves, they will not achieve equality in America. He came at last to the main point. "It is better for both of us then to be separated," Lincoln said, adding that "there is an unwillingness on the part of our people, harsh as it may be, for you free colored people to remain with us."

The President did not expect any argument from his guests. These were five freedmen from Washington, D.C., especially picked for this occasion. Lincoln hoped that through them his "interview" and his plan would receive wide and favorable publicity among black people, slave and free.

He was proposing an experiment. A body of Negroes would be sent to a place called Chiriquí, on the Isthmus of Panama. The President painted for his guests a glowing picture of this tropical land, adding, however, that there would be many hardships. The blacks going to Chiriquí would work for mine owners, digging coal which was to be purchased by the United States Navy. The President concluded with a bit of poetry, and the interview was over.

The idea of exporting Negroes was not new—it had, in fact, been a favorite notion of Thomas Jefferson. Nor was Lincoln a newcomer to this plan. In his earlier years, he had supported a movement to send free Negroes to Africa.

Lincoln, however, was the first President to make the exporting of Negroes an official policy of the government. And Chiriquí was only the first of many such programs which he had in mind.

Step two in Lincoln's three-fold strategy came within ten days. The first black troops were inducted into the Union army. A call for Negro volunteers was posted in the Union-held sea-islands of South Carolina. Five regiments of black soldiers were quickly formed, trained, and thrown into battle. Their first great victories were to come the following spring, when several Confederate strongholds would fall under their fierce assault.

Meanwhile, Lincoln turned to his third step—emancipation. To a special meeting of the Cabinet on September 22, 1862, the President brought a "preliminary" proclamation.

It was written as an open threat to the Confederacy: if they did not lay down their arms within one hundred days, the slaves would be declared free. In the document, Lincoln restated his plan to "colonize persons of African descent, with their consent, upon this continent, or elsewhere."

Lincoln's bold triple move had its desired effect. It confused many of the President's abolitionist critics; it calmed those white people who feared that the country would be "overrun" with freed blacks; and it strengthened the Union position in the war.

The colonization plan of President Lincoln was greeted by Negroes with mixed feelings. Among black people there were always some voices which spoke out for complete separation of the races. In fact, this trend would rise again and again whenever the cause of freedom in America appeared hopeless and white racism impossible to change. Black Americans would dream of finding a homeland in Africa or elsewhere or of building a separate nation on some part of American soil which they could call their own.

During the Civil War, life in the North had actually worsened for the black man. Regardless of their eagerness to work for the Union cause, Negroes were a despised minority, beset by racial prejudice, gripped by extreme poverty. In a series of wartime mob riots, white workers in the seaboard cities lynched black men in the streets and invaded their homes.

Embittered, some freedmen agreed to the colonization plans. They saw no hope for themselves in a land which showed few signs of ever acknowledging their humanness. In addition to Lincoln's government projects, similar private schemes were already sending thousands of blacks to Africa and to the Caribbean islands.

However, the great majority of Negroes rejected colonization. "Why this desire to get rid of us?" asked one Negro newspaper. "Can it be possible that the nation has robbed us for nearly two and a half centuries, and finds she can do it no longer?" A New Jersey freedman asked the President pointedly, "Is our right to a home in this country less than your own?"

At no time did Lincoln propose that Negroes become settlers on the vast government lands in the West. Nor did he suggest any plan to parcel out to former slaves the huge plantations of the South that might be confiscated after a Union victory. Freedmen pointed out repeatedly that Lincoln's colonial plan veiled a deep belief in the inferiority of black people. The idea, they said, stemmed from the false doctrine that the Negro was forever incapable of becoming a citizen in a self-governing nation.

The Emancipation Proclamation, when it came on January 1, 1863, was greeted with joyous acclaim by blacks in the North and with half-hidden jubilation among the slaves in the Confederate South. However, blacks were not at that time granted citizenship or the right to vote. Emancipation failed to abolish slavery in the Border States. The decree did omit the reference to colonization—even though Lincoln went ahead with his plans.

Another year passed before colonization was revealed as a grim and utter failure. The coal in the Chiriquí mines proved to be "as nearly worthless as any fuel can be." It turned out that another of Lincoln's new colonies, in Haiti, was run by a swindler, who robbed the black migrants of their meager funds, leaving them stranded on a barren island. Starvation and smallpox took an appalling toll among the thousands who carried their hopes for freedom to distant shores. Malaria and yellow fever added to the numbers of the dead.

In late February 1864 Lincoln sent a hospital ship to bring back the last survivors of his colonial experiment.

Night Riders

With the end of the Civil War and the adoption of the Thirteenth Amendment, slavery was dead. And with it had gone the South's old way of "keeping the black man in his place."

But in the spring of 1867, a group of men gathered secretly in Nashville, Tennessee. They met to deal with the problem of "what to do about Negroes."

These men of the defeated Confederacy had formed a new organization. Its name was so secret that it was not set down in writing. In whispers, the founders agreed on purposes and methods, and swore one another to silence.

Their chosen leader was the Confederate general Nathan Bedford Forrest, a hard-hitting cavalry commander. Forrest had made his fortune as a dealer in slaves. Among his wartime exploits was the capture of the Union garrison at Fort Pillow, Tennessee, held by Negro troops. Forrest took no prisoners. Every black man in the fort was killed.

From the Nashville meeting in 1867, Forrest and his followers went into every southern state. Terror and bloodshed followed in their wake. Black families struggling to farm small plots were burned out. Freedmen who registered to vote were flogged. Local leaders among the former slaves were tortured and killed.

Forrest ruled the dreaded "Invisible Empire" of the Ku Klux Klan, and by the end of the 1860s a half-million violent night riders galloped across the South.

Meanwhile, on the western plains, more drumming hoofbeats echoed America's eastern racial turmoil. The very same troops which took part in a war that ended black slavery were now thrown into another war—against members of another race.

DECADE OF DECISION
"No Question of Honor"

"The only good Indians I ever saw were dead," said General Philip H. Sheridan in 1869. And it explained why his cavalry a year later was riding hard against Indians all across the American West.

The remark summed up an attitude taken by white men not long after they began arriving on this continent. They found here a people who were not Christians, who spoke a strange language, held to unfamiliar customs, and steadfastly refused to be enslaved. Obviously, they were members of another race. To the whites, the Indians were plainly "inferior."

The white newcomers to this land hardly acted as guests and made no pretense to good behavior. They took what they wanted without asking. And they became indignant when the "redskins" turned unfriendly. Indians were seen as members of a "savage race," to be tamed or destroyed by the "superior" white men. The new arrivals quickly demonstrated the superiority of their weapons. Warfare spread across the American frontier. If the Indians proved less deadly than the white men, they were at least as fierce in defense of their homelands.

In colonial wars between the French and the English, Indians fought on either side and were paid for white men's scalps. However, a bounty on Indian scalps was offered by almost every colony. And this practice continued in New England long after the American Revolution.

It was not until the year 1814 that Indiana gave up its cash rewards for the scalps of the very people for whom the territory was named. The bounty had been given as "an encouragement to the enterprise and bravery of our fellow citizens." In 1866, Arizona was still paying $250 for each Apache scalp.

In the post–Civil War years, black men and Indians in America were on almost equal terms. Neither were citizens or voters. They were generally considered to be members of inferior races. Both groups were outcasts from white society, victims of prejudice and race violence. Former black slaves who had fought valiantly in the Civil War were the victims of unkept promises. The Indian natives of this land, suffering from no less than four hundred broken treaties, also had serious doubts about the white man's integrity.

Steadily, the Indian was being pushed out of his homeland. By fraud or force, he lost his birthright. The command came out of the muzzle of a gun: "Move!" Farther and farther westward the tribes drifted, beyond the Mississippi. But here, too, the Indian was in the way of plowing teams or track-laying crews. Wherever the fugitive paused, he drew the fire of the white migrants, greedy for the land, its timber, minerals, crops.

"This Anglo-Saxon race will not allow the train of civilization to stop," warned an official government report. "If the Indian in his wildness plants himself on the track, he must inevitably be crushed by it."

The Indian fought back, losing ground steadily. Occasional fierce counterraids gained him nothing but more white vengeance. He was hounded by the army, a relentless and overwhelming force. Most frustrating were his dealings with the government, which used polite language but "spoke with a forked tongue."

Official Washington hardly made any pretense of good

faith. "When dealing with savage men, as with savage beasts," declared the United States Commissioner of Indian Affairs, General Francis G. Walker, "no question of national honor can arise."

At the time, the Indians were classified as *Homo Americanus,* a wild species native to this continent. Many whites regarded them as they did the cougar and the grizzly bear, which were also fighting for their existence.

When people are thought to be less than human, their lives are in danger. The "red" race was considered fair game. For one Topeka, Kansas, newspaper the Indians were "a set of miserable, dirty, lousy, blanketed, thieving, lying, sneaking, murdering, graceless, faithless, gut-eating skunks, whose immediate and final extermination all men should pray for."

The Indian was, in fact, dying a slow death. His ancestral lands represented not only survival, but also his heritage and his religion. He himself belonged to the land—and without it life seemed to lose its meaning. The one thing to which he could still cling was the tribe. This, for the Indian, was some basis of strength, a government of his own through which he could deal with the white men's government.

In the autumn of 1871 came a crushing blow. Congress decreed that no Indian tribe "shall be acknowledged as an independent nation, tribe or power, with whom the United States may contract by treaty." The Indians were now individual wards of the federal government, shorn of their unity. The official edict took away the remaining source of the Indian's dignity as a tribal member of a once-proud people.

The tragedy was hardly recognized by most white Americans. Among those who did take notice were a handful of scientists who had begun to probe a new field. Social anthropologists, as they called themselves, were studying nothing less than man himself, his social patterns and groupings, his works, and ways of life.

In America, the anthropologists were a small group. They had not yet undertaken the serious study of men as members of various societies and cultures. However, a few bold adventurers were moving toward new horizons of human knowledge.

One of them trudged the dusty trails of the Indian territories, asking questions in halting tribal speech, endlessly filling notebooks. His name was Morgan.

Indian Lore

The small-town folks among whom Lewis Henry Morgan grew up could afford to think kindly about the American Indians, who had all but vanished. The Indians had retreated into the backwoods of upstate New York, silenced and dimly seen.

Once, white men and proud Iroquois had fought bitterly in these valleys. But the last rifle volley and the last war whoop had long since died away. And the fierce tribesmen lived only as fabled and romantic figures in the stories of old men and in the games of small boys.

Morgan was a member of an ambitious and aggressive generation in mid-century America, then a fast-growing, westward-moving nation. At the time he finished college, young Lewis held the typical white man's attitudes toward black men and Indians. "Primitives" and "savages" were his words for them—while he saw himself and his race as bearers of "civilization."

In Rochester, New York, he was a lawyer by profession

and a scholar by choice. A sober, bookish young man with a stubborn jaw, Lewis Morgan never seemed able to let well enough alone. Even in the fraternal lodge to which he belonged, Morgan was not content simply to go through the usual kinds of secret rituals and to dress up in fancy costumes. His lodge called itself The Grand Order of the Iroquois. As president, Morgan began to study the actual customs and traditions of the five Iroquois nations.

His interests led him into a close friendship with a young law student, an Iroquois Indian whose father was chief of the Seneca tribe. The Senecas held land by an old treaty near the city of Buffalo, but promoters were trying to clear them out in order to build a commercial development. The policy of Indian removal was being carried on vigorously across the nation. Tribal lands were being taken over by one means or another wherever white men wanted them.

The Buffalo land company used tactics which were hardly novel. A group of Indians were brought to a hotel room, "elected" Seneca chiefs, and presented with a small amount of money. In exchange, the bogus chiefs signed a new treaty which gave up the tribal lands.

Outraged when he heard this story, Morgan summoned his Grand Order of the Iroquois and fellow lawyers onto the legal warpath. Few Indians had ever had such a court defense as that staged by Morgan and his warriors. In the law courts and in the capital, the battle for the Senecas was waged and won. After victory, Morgan was a regular guest at Iroquois functions and a devoted student of Indian lore.

On a late autumn night in the year 1846, the young lawyer sat at a great council fire. Four days of ceremony and dance were ending quietly with prayers of thanks to the Great Spirit for the harvest. It was a night filled with moonglow, the wind swirling the dry birch and maple leaves. On the lake's edge, Morgan watched enchanted while the Indians repeated the rites handed down by generations of Iroquois. In the firelight, the lawyer jotted as rapidly as he could, noting every detail.

That night the Iroquois had prepared a special honor for the white guest who was so deeply absorbed in their customs. Morgan was brought before the array of elders. With great pomp and dignity, he was adopted into the tribe and given the tribal name of *Ta-ya-da-o-wuh-kuh,* meaning "one lying across." The elders explained to Morgan that they viewed him as a bridge between the Indian and white races.

During the next years Morgan was absorbed in a systematic study of all phases of Iroquois life—customs, laws, myths, languages, forms of self-government. He probed Indian courtship and marriage, mourning and celebration, the styles of work and play. A side interest had now become a serious venture into science.

The so-called American School of Anthropology was in those years concerned with classifying members of various races. Like the skull specialist, Dr. Samuel G. Morton, others were busy with magnifiers and calipers. They argued over human measurements, differed over the various skin colors, split up over the varied thicknesses and qualities of hair, took sides on the numbers of existing races.

Morgan shunned that kind of anthropology. He had become an expert writer and lecturer on Indian life. It was Morgan who helped museums develop their collections of Indian relics. But he was primarily a field worker who repeatedly returned to the Indian trails and the tribal villages.

He was an odd figure on the American frontier. In his hard collar, sideburns, and waistcoat, he could be seen wandering in the West, far from the coach and train routes, a lone white man in the Indian country. Since he was pioneering in a young field of science, many of Morgan's ideas would be questioned by later research. But there was no doubt that he was exploring new ground.

Morgan poured his immense knowledge into a book called *The League of the Iroquois*. Blazing a new trail, the book was the first scientific account ever written of Indian life.

In a time when almost all white Americans were blinded by hatred for members of other races, Morgan attempted to reveal the Indians in a new light. He realized that over many centuries they had developed special ways of life—a distinct and valuable culture, or a variety of cultures. Foreseeing how future anthropologists would view human societies, Morgan pointed out that if the scientific truth about a people is to be found, "it must be sought in their customs and institutions."

Morgan was amazed at the well-developed forms of self-government which he found in Indian tribes. Their societies were relatively free of crime. Within the tribe they shared both their hardship and their bounty. In studying the history of the Iroquois confederation before the coming of the whites, Morgan found that this "is perhaps the only league of nations ever instituted among men which can point to three centuries of uninterrupted unity and peace."

Morgan's law practice now involved him deeply in railroad and mining ventures. He found himself a part of the expanding business interests that were pushing the tribes out of their homes to make way for "progress."

Although an avowed friend of the Indian, the anthropologist was never quite able to shake himself loose from the bigotry of his own background. Often, he judged "red men" by white men's values. The Indians were dying out, thought Morgan, by failing to adopt the white man's way of life. "Race has yielded to race," he wrote, "the inevitable result of the contact of the civilized with the hunter life."

And yet, there were moments when Morgan seemed to overcome the prevailing attitudes of racial superiority. Although the Indian "has never contributed a page to science, not a discovery to art," the anthropologist remarked, "still there are qualities of his mind which shine forth in all the lustre of natural perfection."

But in the 1870s white America was in no mood to listen to reason. The country was trained to hear only the grisly tales of Indian savagery, with the United States Cavalry thundering bravely to the rescue of defenseless white men, women, and children. The old drama was soon to have its most stirring rerun.

A Broken Treaty

The Black Hills of South Dakota were sacred earth. To generations of Indians, the snowy peaks were a temple. And the silent valleys, which contained their ancient dead, were held in reverence.

In the 1868 Treaty of Fort Laramie, the Sioux had received the solemn oath of the United States government that it would never trespass on their hallowed ground. But white men, who had nothing but contempt for the Indians, had little regard for their religion. Besides, the Black Hills in these years had taken on the glitter of gold. The precious metal had been discovered in the region.

In the Great Plains, the federal government in the 1870s had begun its most determined campaign to smash the remaining centers of Indian strength. Army assaults were carried on against villages and "hostile" bands. By continuous harassment whole tribes were starved out, deprived of their traditional hunting livelihood. The buffalo, a major resource of the Plains Indian, was being wiped out by deliberate plan. Once, these plains had held vast concentrations of these massive beasts, which served the Indian not only as food but for a large variety of other uses. Between the years 1870 and 1872, the main herds were destroyed. The United States Army accounted for part of the slaughter. Professional hunters were paid by the railroads to bring down thousands of the animals. So-called sportsmen finished the job.

A favorite pastime for train passengers was firing into the herds from the railroad coaches. Several rail lines advertised this attraction to brighten up a tiresome journey.

To the Sioux tribes, it seemed as though they were under siege. From the Black Hills, they were driven westward toward the Bighorn Mountains. The Northern Pacific Railroad was extending its line across Sioux territory. And with it, the Indians knew, would come white settlements.

The year 1876 brought gold prospectors swarming into the region. Mining companies demanded in Washington that they be permitted to operate freely in the Indian country, regardless of treaties. One of their spokesmen, a Colorado congressman, argued that "an idle and thriftless race of savages cannot be permitted to guard the treasure vaults of the nation which hold our gold and silver!"

On a June day of that year, a column of United States cavalry paused in its hunt "for the enemy." A scout reported signs of enough Sioux for two or three days' fighting. "In that case," scoffed the cavalry commander, "We'll finish them off in one day."

The officer was General George Armstrong Custer, a brash, young veteran of the Civil War and ten years of campaigning against the Indians. His Seventh Cavalry was a part of a large striking force, escorting gold prospectors into the Black Hills. Their military orders were not to defend but to attack.

Still in his thirties, Custer was a cocky and colorful military man to whom this war against the Indians was like a wild game hunt. He wore his yellow hair in ringlets, dressed in sand-colored buckskins, and sometimes he dared Indian sharpshooters by wearing a bright red shirt.

Custer was known among his troops to be swaggering, boastful, ambitious. He wrote up his exploits and sent them off to newspapers and magazines. His personal goals were now political, as well as military. He noted carefully that two generals, Jackson and Harrison, had become President of the United States on their reputations as Indian fighters.

One of his superiors described Custer as "cold-blooded." The Indians called him squaw-killer, a merciless butcher who wiped out whole villages. Against tribesmen armed with rifles or with bows and arrows, Custer used rapid-fire weapons and three-inch cannon.

It was a sleeping tepee village that Custer saw that June morning over a rim of a river bluff. The village was large enough to make Custer wonder briefly whether he should call for help from other army units deployed nearby. There was safety in greater numbers—but glory in going it alone. Custer went to the attack on the Sioux force encamped along the river known as the Little Bighorn. The battle lasted no more than a half hour. When it was over Custer was dead, along with 264 of his men.

The news came eastward at a bad time. Word of Custer's defeat arrived on July 4, just as the United States was celebrating the one-hundredth anniversary of the Declaration of Independence. Caught up in patriotic fervor, many Americans cried out for vengeance against the Indians.

Orators in Congress and elsewhere made a martyr of Custer, and newspapers trumpeted open hatred against "savages of an evil race."

One voice, barely heard, asked the question: "Who shall blame the Sioux for defending themselves, their wives and their children, when attacked in their own encampment and threatened with destruction?" The query was that of the anthropologist Lewis Henry Morgan. He sensed that what was called Custer's Last Stand in reality marked the last feeble defense of the Plains Indians.

Night of Terror

Exactly a century had passed since America declared that "all men are created equal." And in the village of Hamburg, South Carolina, July 4, 1876, was a day to be remembered.

The heat of the holiday afternoon hung in simmering waves. A small parade swung through the broad main street. Its chief feature was a local troop of black militia, dressed in their Civil War uniforms.

Suddenly, a horse and buggy appeared, meeting the marching men face to face. Reining up, the white driver shouted wildly for the militia to get out of his way. The black officer in charge suggested that the buggy could pass with plenty of room to spare. From the two young white men came angry insults—and a threat that they would return.

When they came back, it was in the company of a large, heavily armed force of white Confederate veterans gathered up from the surrounding towns. After a quick exchange of rifle fire, the twenty-one black militiamen were forced to take cover in a brick warehouse. Their ammunition was soon gone, and they found themselves surrounded by an overwhelming force. The attackers had brought in heavy artillery.

By nightfall, several of the Negro townsmen were dead. Others were shot as they tried to escape from the besieged warehouse. The rest were taken prisoner. The white men enjoyed tormenting their captives for a time. Before the victors left, the black prisoners were shot in cold blood.

The Hamburg massacre was not strange or unusual. It was a link in a chain of similar violence across the South. New shackles were being prepared for the black people who had been so recently freed.

In the ten years that had followed the end of the Civil War, a kind of democracy was briefly enforced in the South. The former Confederate states were occupied by Union troops. Their bayonets upheld the federal laws which provided that black men as well as white were now permitted to vote. The result was that for the first time Negroes were elected as officials on many levels of government. Blacks from the South served ably in both houses of Congress. Former slaves administered high state offices. Blacks as well as whites were elected to conventions which rebuilt the shattered state governments. With blacks casting their first ballots, men were chosen for office who expressed concern for the needs of the common people. Reforms were carried out in education, welfare, care for the aged and the sick. Democracy was broadened in the South as laws were enacted to benefit poor people, black and white.

In South Carolina, black legislators helped bring about sweeping changes. Every new reform law, each expenditure, every break with the slavery past was cursed by the adherents of the Old South, steeped in anti-Negro hatred. But federal troops patrolled the state Capitol at Columbia, and the Legislature carried on its business.

By 1876, the former slaveholders had regained some of

their wealth. Many of the big plantations were again in operation. The new middle class of the South was extending its power.

That year, the nation carried out its strangest presidential election. The two opposing candidates were both Northerners—Republican Rutherford B. Hayes of Ohio and Samuel J. Tilden, a New York Democrat.

Months after the balloting the outcome was still in doubt. The results in three southern states were in dispute. Without these electoral votes decided, neither of the two candidates could be declared the winner.

The deadlock was broken by what the history books later called the Hayes-Tilden Compromise. This was an election finally settled by men behind closed doors, trading in railroad subsidies, tariff laws, political jobs—and the rights of black people in the South.

Hayes was finally declared the winner. But in return for giving him the margin of victory, southern white leaders made some harsh demands. Hayes agreed to withdraw the remaining federal troops who were stationed in the South to protect the voting rights of freedmen. Black people were suddenly thrown to the mercy of the former slave masters.

The Union troops had hardly left for home before a rebel yell of vengeance was heard across the South. Voting by blacks was soon to be halted by trickery or by terror. The violence of Hamburg was repeated all across the South.

The South Carolina massacre had, in fact, spawned white leaders of a new type. There were two men who had led the assault against the Hamburg villagers. One was Confederate General Matthew C. Butler. He became the United States senator from South Carolina that year. The other leader of the riot was Benjamin Tillman. After serving as governor, he would become the strident voice of the South in the United States Senate.

THE EIGHTEEN EIGHTIES
"Survival of the Fittest"

Benjamin Tillman liked to be called Pitchfork Ben. The South Carolinian was a rich farmer, but he preferred to be known as a poor one.

In his thrust for power, Tillman was driven by seething hatred. He had come out of the red-soil cottonlands, a planter and slaveowner. Following the Civil War, he had seen his former slaves go to the polling places in a region where blacks outnumbered whites two to one.

Ben Tillman never forgot the trembling panic that overcame him in those years. His fear of Negroes deformed him into a twisted man, given to violence and fits of temper. He was the first of what was to become a familiar type of politician—the Dixie demagogue, a fire-eating, foul-talking, rabble-rousing dealer in race hatred.

The South in the 1880s was a region where common folk lived in extreme poverty. After the Civil War, both black and white struggled for a meager living as fieldhands and millhands, tenants and sharecroppers. Members of both races were dirt farmers, grubbing small plots of poor land, barely making ends meet.

It might have seemed that poor whites would have made common cause with poor blacks, uniting for their own joint interests. But race prejudice stood in the way. A barrier of towering hatred turned the poverty-stricken white population of the South into bitter enemies of the black people. Poor whites added their numbers to the raiding Ku Klux Klan bands and the lynch mobs.

Their spokesman was Ben Tillman, who became a dominant figure in southern politics. It was Tillman who rode at the head of the Red Shirts, the South Carolina variety of the Klan. And Tillman took the lead in putting an end to black voting in South Carolina.

The mere suggestion of any challenge to white power was enough to send Tillman into a frenzy, his face blood-red and his voice shrieking sinister curses. What riled him most was the idea that the Negro had a vote which was exactly equal to that of a white man.

"We took the vote away from them," he later boasted on the floor of the Senate. "We stuffed ballot boxes. We shot them! We are not ashamed of it!"

Tillman put himself on record as justifying lynching or any other means to put the Negro "in his place." He delighted in goading northern senators to respond to his tirades of bigotry. In a sneering reply, Tillman then challenged the legislators to prove that they had made life in the North more endurable for black people. As a rule, Pitchfork Ben had the last word.

Tillman was a pillar of what became known as the Solid South. This was one-party rule. Whatever contests took place were held within the privacy of the Democratic party primary—and black voters were barred.

For decades to come, northern political leaders were to come to terms with the Solid South. In the Senate Tillman and his colleagues were able to block any federal civil rights laws. But white leaders from North and South were usually able to settle their differences amicably—at the expense of the Negro people.

In the northern cities, blacks had long suffered under a system of racial segregation to which the South gave the name "Jim Crow." In its southern version, Jim Crow became a total way of life.

Jim Crow

If white Americans in the 1880s had any dissenting thoughts about race, they kept mum. Racial prejudice was the fashion of the day, North and South, in the salons of high society and in the poor-white saloons across the tracks.

Black people, some only recently released from bondage, had by this time revealed their abilities—as poets and educators, as scientists and statesmen. But white America seemed to take an even tighter grip on its idea of Negro inferiority.

Scientists had begun to cast some doubt on the old-fashioned view of race. But most "Caucasians" would admit to nothing. If the black man was not born "inferior," the trend of the times was to try to make him so—by conditioning. If the Negro had no shortcomings at his moment of birth, his lifetime experiences would gradually make him subordinate to the white man.

This was the idea behind Jim Crow. It was designed not merely to divide the races from each other. More important, the plan was to separate black people from the benefits of American life. Poor education and limited opportunities, reduced income and low standards of living, greater health hazards as well as a shorter life span—these were to be the Negro's lot.

The code of Jim Crow was carried out strictly and thoroughly. The rules were laid down by law, enforced by violence, proclaimed by thousands of signs which were posted throughout the South. "Colored" and "Whites Only" were the warnings seen everywhere—at water fountains, pay windows, waiting rooms, toilets, public parks, hospitals, cemeteries.

From the cradle to the grave, the two races lived separated lives. South Carolina law forbade black and white laborers from working in the same room. The courts in Atlanta furnished two sets of Jim Crow Bibles for witnesses. In North Carolina and Virginia, the law said that members of both races could not join any church or group where people addressed one another as Brother.

Double facilities were built and maintained at a staggering cost to citizens of both races. But Jim Crow was not merely the drawing of the color line. In every case, black people received the worst and the least of everything, the unwanted and the left over—or nothing at all.

In the South, blacks could be found only in the back of the coach and in the gallery of the theater, in the unheated waiting room and in the windowless hospital room. Often the black portion of town had no fire protection and no water supply. The Negro was barred from white labor unions. He could not buy insurance or use the public library.

The southern states spent little for public education. Their schools for white children were the worst in the nation—except for their schools for black children. Where they existed at all, the so-called Negro schools offered the least possible education. It was the firm belief of southern whites that the schooling of Negroes was "a waste of time and money."

For violating the Jim Crow code, a black man, woman, or child could go to jail or fall into the clutches of a lynch mob. By 1882, lynching had become such a regular occurrence that the federal government took to keeping an official tally.

Most often, a lynching began with the real or imagined refusal of a black man to observe the Jim Crow rules or to bow to the "superiority" of the white race. He might have attempted to vote or to join a union. Or perhaps he was "disrespectful" to a white man or woman. For such reasons, blacks were lynched at the rate of two or three each week. Seldom were lynchings simple, cold-blooded executions. The victim, in fact, would be lucky to be put to death quickly.

Often a lynching "bee" became a public outing, whole families thronging to watch the spectacle. While the majority of white Americans hardly approved of lynching, still there was no sharp public outcry of protest.

A few people were aware of how racial bigotry had made Americans increasingly callous to the sufferings of their fellow men. One of these was the writer Mark Twain. The book he began writing in 1882, *Huckleberry Finn*, was full of rich humor. It also contained some wry comments on the narrow-minded sense of decency and mercy among so many white Americans.

In the coarse, racist speech of the time, Twain described Huck reporting to Aunt Sally on a steamboat accident. Her response was, "Good gracious! Anybody hurt?"

"No'm. Killed a nigger."

"Well, it's lucky; because sometimes people do get hurt."

Darwin Distorted

A shadowy form had begun to appear out of ancient times. Anthropologists specializing in man's origins had dug up a great many bones, the ages of which were revealed by the layers of earth in which they were found.

From prehistoric fossils, the scientists reconstructed a bandy-legged, heavy-jawed, low-browed man with a slight stoop. He apparently had a good-sized brain, made tools, hunted, lived in caves, and buried his dead. By the 1880s similar skeletons were found in many European sites, but also in the Middle East, and in the Far East as well.

The discoveries offered some idea of the types of men and manlike beings who had preceded modern man. The prehuman types being unearthed showed clearly that man had not descended from apes or from any other species of animal now existing.

The fossil record had begun to prove the theories of Charles Darwin. However, as always, there seemed to be a lag between scientific discovery and the concepts that persisted in the public mind.

Darwin died in the year 1882. The popular version of his theory that survived him offered little understanding of the meaning of human races. In the simple, commonly held view of the age, Darwin's theory was that man had descended from apes. And neither the British biologist nor his fellow scientists had ever been able to correct that false notion.

In America, professional racists used what they called Darwinism to prop up a new view of race. The Negro, they said, was the "missing link" between man and ape. A flood of literature appeared in those years setting forth this doctrine. It was nonsense masquerading as science, falsehood posing as fact.

In the name of Darwin, an ominous social theory was beginning to take hold as well. The great biologist had seemed to suggest in *Origin of Species* that all living things were engaged in a struggle for "the survival of the fittest." In a manner that Darwin never intended, that idea was molded into a ready-made justification for a great variety of things—such as war, poverty, colonialism, race hatred, and the fate of oppressed peoples.

The theory became known as Social Darwinism. It was,

in fact, a misleading way of applying Darwin's view of nature to human society.

The Social Darwinists championed an aggressive and warlike point of view. In most respects their ideas were at complete odds with those of Darwin. The British biologist pictured mankind, as well as other species, in a struggle to overcome the problems of environment. The Social Darwinists emphasized the struggle of man against man.

If animals prey on each other, said the doctrine of Social Darwinism, human societies and human races do the same. The promoters of this belief held that according to "natural law," man's world was a kind of jungle in which the strongest inevitably became rich and dominant.

The poor are poor and the weak are weak because they were born inferior, they argued, and those nations and races that rule the world are naturally those that are more fit to do so.

The theory was not Darwinism. Nor was it science. In fact, it was based on a misunderstanding of nature in the wild, where plant and animal species do not ordinarily destroy each other but tend to live together in stable communities. As Darwin stressed, there is cooperation in nature as well as competition. Moreover, survival is not based on brute strength alone but on the ability of a species or a race or an organism to adapt well to the conditions of its life. Because this is true, some of the most powerful predatory types of beasts have become extinct, while certain fragile plants and delicate animal species have thrived through the ages.

The greatest error of Social Darwinism was that it tried to blot out the differences that exist between nature's wilderness and human societies. The brain of man clearly set him off from the wilderness, even though his origins were in that world. The human mind had created cultures and languages, religions and arts, sciences and philosophies. Man had a conscience to deal with, a developed sense of right and wrong, an urge toward a more peaceful, more free, more democratic way of life.

But Social Darwinism was cooked up to the tastes of the times. Flavored with a smattering of "science," this hash of half-truths was served up along with white supremacy. It was just the dish for an age of extreme racial bigotry.

Whites, the popular formula went, were the superior, the "fit." Without exception, all others were the inferior, the "unfit." No wonder that whenever race met race on American soil, the tragic results were much the same.

Muscle for Hire

It was no different when the first Chinese began arriving in San Francisco Bay. The discovery of gold in 1849 had turned the coastal town disorderly and lawless. The harbor was choked with incoming ships. From every vessel, men jumped ashore to vie with those who had come before them for bits of precious metal.

The immigrant Chinese who were shipped to the California gold fields came not as private prospectors. They were contract laborers, imported by companies engaged in mining. Little more than slaves, the Chinese worked off the debt for their passage. They were *k'u-li*, the Chinese term meaning "muscle for hire," unskilled labor.

Their employers set brutal and ill-paid conditions of work. Quickly enough, the Chinese learned from the rest of the Californians that they were unwelcome. The newcomers found that here they were members of a loathed race.

The railroads used thousands of Chinese for the heavy work of laying the tracks across the deserts and through the mountains. So-called coolies moved between the mining camps, the railroad construction sites, and the narrow, crowded, segregated Chinatowns that grew up in every coastal city.

In a vicious circle of hatred, the whites denounced them as members of an alien race, who showed little desire to become Christians and refused to adopt the white man's customs, dress, or speech.

The Chinese found little here but suffering and abuse. They were brutally beaten and often lynched by white mobs. In 1871 came the first of many similar riots. Almost the entire white population of Los Angeles joined in the hanging of twenty-two Chinese in the center of town. Wherever they competed for jobs with white labor, the Chinese paid heavily with their lives. Into American speech came the phrase, "a Chinaman's chance," meaning no chance at all.

Barred from the polls, the Chinese were also denied the use of the courts. The California Supreme Court applied to the Chinese the same state law which declared that "no Black, or Mulatto person, or Indian shall be allowed to give evidence in favor of, or against, a white man."

In its decision, the high court described the Chinese as

> a race of people whom nature has marked as inferior, and who are incapable of progress or intellectual development beyond a certain point, as their history has shown; differing in language, opinion, color, and physical conformation; between whom and ourselves nature has placed an impassable difference.

Stirred up by the white dockworkers in San Francisco, a powerful hate movement succeeded in ending Chinese immigration to America. This was the first time any ethnic group had been barred from these shores. In demanding that Congress exclude the Chinese, the official representative from the city of San Francisco testified in Washington: "The Chinese are inferior to any race God ever made. . . . I believe the Chinese have no souls, and if they have, they are not worth saving."

The more they were shunned and mistreated, the more the Chinese kept to themselves. Most planned to return to China once they had paid for their passage and earned a little extra money. But this only brought down on them further condemnation.

On a single day in 1885, members of two racial groups—Chinese and Indians—linked together as Mongoloids in the mists of past ages, found themselves under attack in the Wyoming Territory. In the Sweetwater Basin, Sioux and Cheyenne tribes were being harassed by United States Cavalry.

Not far away, in the mining camp at Rock Springs, all was quiet that late evening. A white mob had done its work and departed. In the silent village, twenty-nine Chinese lay dead, their belongings scattered, their homes destroyed.

TEN JINGO YEARS
"Don't You Wish That You Were Me?"

In the year 1890, the embattled American Indian was busy keeping a sharp lookout for pale-faced enemies. He learned that he had better keep watch on white "friends" as well.

"The sad plight of the red man" had come to the attention of well-meaning folk back East. Many were sincere and helpful, trying to end what was called "a century of dishonor." Others made believe they were helping the Indian —by helping themselves to his land.

Under the guise of reforming United States policy, Congress had passed the Dawes Act of 1887. Even if the law was really meant to assist them, the Indians learned three years later that it spelled disaster.

Some Americans were openly trying to exterminate the "red man." The supporters of the Dawes Act were just as eager to make him disappear—by turning him into a white man.

In those years, the small farmer, independent and hardworking, was considered to be the model American citizen. The Dawes Act attempted to transform the Plains Indian into just such a farmer.

The plan called for breaking up all the Indian tribal lands into plots averaging 160 acres. Each Indian would be given a farmstead, where supposedly he would live and work the rest of his life, forsaking Indian customs and tribal attachments, his heritage and his beliefs. The sponsors of the new law argued that he would be "swallowed up" in the white world, and thereby his problems would be solved.

By 1890, few Indians had shown any desire to become a part of this scheme. Those who did found that while the plan gave them land, they had no money with which to buy livestock, equipment, seed, buildings, fencing. The western land available to them was poor. Its thin soil, once it had been broken by the plow, would vanish quickly in dust and erosion. This was a region without enough rainfall to support small-scale crop farming.

The announced goal of the government was to end the age-old Indian practice of holding tribal lands in common. In its effect, the Dawes plan stripped from the Indians what remained of their large land holdings. The total acreage allotted to the Indian accounted for only a tiny portion of the original tribal territory. The rest of the land was declared surplus and sold. Within a year or two, whites outnumbered Indians six to one on former Indian reservations. Moreover, the whites held the best of the land.

The stark injustice in the Dawes plan arose not merely from the dishonesty of the government agents who carried it out or from the greed of the white settlers. At bottom, this law viewed the Indians as an inferior race, representing a useless culture and a worthless set of values. The law tried to force them into an alien way of life, to make of them something they never wanted to be.

Unlike the white settler with a centuries-old tradition of European farming, the tribesman had no interest in a lonely life of farm drudgery, confined to a small piece of infertile land, at the mercy of white speculators, bankers, and merchants.

His roots were in tribal life, which the Dawes Act was clearly out to destroy. "The idea," explained the Massachusetts senator who wrote the law, "is to take the Indians out one by one from under the tribe . . . and then, before the tribe is aware of it, its existence as a tribe is gone."

Apparently, neither the senator nor anyone else in the government had made a sincere effort to find out whether the Indian wanted such a program. One man who might have given them some invaluable guidance was the old Sioux chief Sitting Bull.

It was Sitting Bull who had spoken out most clearly about tragic Indian dealings with "another race, small and feeble when our fathers first met them, but now great and overbearing."

The old chief said of the whites:

Strangely enough, they have a mind to till the soil, and the love of possession is a disease with them. These people have made many rules that the rich may break but the poor may not. They take tithes from the poor and weak to support the rich and those who rule. They claim this mother of ours, the earth, for their own and fence their neighbors away; they deface her with their buildings and their refuse. That nation is like a spring freshet that overruns its banks and destroys all who are in its path.

In December 1890 the aged Sitting Bull was arrested as a "troublemaker." While in government custody, he was mysteriously killed.

In bitterness and despair, the Plains Indians in that year of 1890 turned to a frenzied kind of religious worship. The Ghost Dance swept through the Sioux tribes. To the throb of drums, tribesmen chanted fervent prayers for survival and the return of a life that the Indians knew before the white man's coming.

United States Army commanders grew alarmed at the reports of these religious ceremonies. The day after Christmas, troops were commanded to search out the dancing tribes.

The Seventh Cavalry, once commanded by General Custer, rounded up several hundred Sioux families in a hollow near Wounded Knee Creek, in South Dakota. Suddenly, the cavalry opened up with field guns and rapid-fire weapons at point-blank range. Some of the Indians ran, but few escaped.

A blizzard had begun, and the dead were left where they lay, freezing in grotesque postures. Several days later, the bodies were gathered up in wagons.

The tribe was one of those which had refused to be split up by the Dawes plan. In that frosty nightfall the tribe lay buried in a common grave.

A Young Man's Hopes

In just such a winter's night in 1893, a young American student in Berlin, Germany, stargazed and scrawled into his diary an account of his twenty-fifth birthday.

"I awoke at eight and took coffee and oranges, read letters, thought of my parents, sang, cried. . . ."

His name was a big mouthful. But the world would know him in time as W. E. B. Du Bois. A Negro scholar from Massachusetts, Du Bois was the kind of person who at twenty-five makes his lifelong plans, and then carries them out.

"Night—grand and wonderful," he wrote, "I am glad I am living. I rejoice as a strong man to run a race." He was a brilliant student, consciously preparing himself to return home to his career, "to work for the rise of the Negro people, taking for granted that their best development means the best development of the world."

"These are my plans," Du Bois carefully recorded, "to make a name in science, to make a name in literature and thus to raise my race. . . ."

In spite of the young man's high hope and purpose, black

people in America were in their worst period since slavery days. The number of lynchings was increasing every year. In the northern cities, a depression hit hardest of all at the poverty-stricken Negro communities.

Negro voting in the South had been virtually ended. Along with the white primary, each southern state had added restrictions—the literacy test, the poll tax, the "grandfather" clause, which limited the vote to those families who had had it during slavery.

The South was drastically cutting the share of education funds allotted to Negro schools. The deliberate effort in miseducating black children was to make them believe that only white Americans had contributed anything of value to this country. Negro children in southern schools were not permitted to use texts which contained the Declaration of Independence or the United States Constitution—lest they learn that they had rights as citizens!

Because the great majority of the black people lived in the South, it often seemed that those states were solely responsible for the problems of the Negro. However, the North also practiced widespread oppression, in slightly different forms.

The Supreme Court repeatedly upheld the unequal treatment of black people. Congress scarcely bothered about the question. Leadership from the White House was nonexistent.

Of the fifteen presidents who had served before the Civil War, ten were slaveholders. Those who followed Lincoln were not enemies of democracy—but while they saw the nation as racially divided and unequal in rights, they did little about it. They led various crusades on political matters, dealt with a wide range of domestic and foreign issues. But not one of these presidents faced up squarely to America's knottiest problem.

In 1896 came the decision called *Plessy* v. *Ferguson*. The Supreme Court upheld the right of railroads to segregate Negro passengers as long as "separate but equal facilities" were provided.

One justice, John M. Harlan, dissented vigorously, declaring that "there can be no doubt that segregation has been enforced as a means of subordinating the Negro." He added, "The thin disguise of equal accommodation will not mislead anyone nor atone for the wrong done this day."

The majority decision of the Supreme Court, however, sounded once again the claim of the "super-race": "If one race be inferior to the other socially, the Constitution of the United States cannot put them on the same plane." Again, the highest court was basing its decision on the doctrine of white supremacy.

A century was slipping into the past. The nation was still in the firm grip of the belief that nature had put races on the rungs of a biological ladder, with Negroes at the bottom.

The coming century would need men like the young scholar Du Bois and many more in order to overturn a wild-growing dogma deeply rooted in falsehood. Meanwhile, the old race theory would continue to flourish and to spread.

Spread Eagle

> Little Indian, Sioux or Crow,
> Little Frosty Eskimo
> Little Turk or Japanee,
> O! don't you wish that you were me?

In the mid-1890s, white American school children were chanting this verse by Robert Louis Stevenson. It somehow fit the mood of the times, of a people filled with arrogance and ready to take on the world.

Increasingly, this nation was becoming impressed with its own importance on the international scene. In the spirit of Social Darwinism, American leaders were urging this country to take its rightful place in the global power struggle. Another ditty of the day went like this:

> We don't want to fight,
> But, by jingo! If we do,
> We've got the ships,
> We've got the men,
> We've got the money, too!

The spirit of "jingo" resulted in an expanded American navy. Its wide-roving vessels were soon coming into war-like encounters with those of other nations. A latecomer in the world rivalry for markets and colonies, the United States seemed ready to try to make up for lost time.

A tiny handful of European nations were then holding in colonial captivity the vast dark-skinned populations of the world. At the end of the nineteenth century, the profits in exploiting colonies were still lavish. The United States was eager to share in the riches—even though the idea of empire building was distasteful to many citizens. The American eagle had begun to spread its wings—and its talons.

A leading American author and editor, William Allen White, urged that the "Anglo-Saxon race" had a duty to perform:

> It is the Anglo-Saxon's manifest destiny to go forth in the world as a world conqueror. He will take possession of all the islands of the sea. He will exterminate the peoples he cannot subjugate. That is what fate holds for the chosen people. It is so written.

Other ideas had also been written. In the year 1895, Frederick Douglass, the venerable black fighter for freedom, died in Washington. He left a rich legacy of struggle, and of wisdom. America was just then entering a period of turmoil which would recall the words of the former slave:

> It is said that the Negro belongs to an inferior race. In-ferior race! This is the apology for all the hell-black crimes ever committed by the white race against the blacks.
>
> Inferior race! It is an old argument used whenever and wherever men have been oppressed and enslaved. When the Normans conquered the Saxons, the Saxons were a coarse, unrefined, inferior race. When the United States wants to possess herself of Mexican territory, the Mexicans are an inferior race. So too, when England wishes to impose some new burden on Ireland, the Irish are denounced as an inferior race. This is a monstrous argument!

This very argument had already been used by white America in enslaving black people, in depriving the Indians of their homelands, in persecuting Chinese coolies, in taking Texas and California from the Mexicans.

The United States, which had pushed out its continental borders in every direction, looked avidly beyond the seas. This was a business-minded nation, seeking raw materials and markets, as well as world power.

In 1896, William E. McKinley was elected President. If he was not ready to lead the jingo parade, at least he wouldn't stand in its way.

Winner Take All

He was a short, stocky man with thin hair and a cleft chin. William E. McKinley, colorless but honest, came out of small-town Ohio politics to find himself President.

McKinley had hardly settled in the Executive Mansion before the empire builders moved in. A close group of senators, military men, and cabinet officers had already plotted an overseas course for the new administration. Hawaii was first in their plans.

Those islands had been under the rule of a native Hawaiian queen. During the previous dozen years, the United States had gradually extended its power in the Hawaiian Islands. Most of the valuable sugar crop had fallen under the control of Americans. The United States Navy held the exclusive use of the base at Pearl Harbor. American residents in Hawaii staged a bloodless coup against the native government—which left little more to do than to hoist the American flag.

Prodded by the jingo group in Washington, President McKinley took the next step. He signed a resolution passed by Congress, taking over the islands.

Cuba was next. The Caribbean island was in the throes of revolt. It was one of the possessions of the once-powerful government of Spain. However, the Spanish empire was clearly crumbling. And many Americans were eager to gather up the pieces.

The newspapers sounded raucous attacks against Spanish colonialism. Congressmen warned that the United States would not tolerate any tyranny in this hemisphere. Free Cuba! became a popular slogan in the United States. Briefly, the bearded rebels in the Cuban hills were pictured as heroes in the American press.

In the late evening of February 15, 1898, the warship *Maine* hit a submarine mine in the Havana harbor, which destroyed the ship and killed 260 Americans aboard. By April 27, the United States was at war with Spain.

Five days later, United States naval forces under Commodore George Dewey sank the Spanish fleet stationed in the harbor of Manila in the Philippine Islands. Dewey's naval victory in Manila Bay caught America, and President McKinley, by surprise. At that moment, he was not even sure until he looked at a globe where the Philippines were located. If he had made a guess, he said, he would have "missed those darned islands by two thousand miles."

Pressed on all sides to grab the Philippines, McKinley hesitated. He was a cautious man. He knew little about the islands. What was the natural setting there? What race inhabited the islands? And how would the "natives" respond to the American presence?

It would be wise, McKinley concluded, to get the advice of experts, including anthropologists. The President appointed an advisory commission and sent them off to the Philippines. Their "scientific" report hardly differed from that of the military men and officers. It was America's "national and racial destiny" to take over the islands, they affirmed. As for the Filipinos, they were "unfit to rule themselves."

Supposedly, the United States had begun its intervention in the Philippines to support the native population, which was rebelling against the colonial rule of Spain. With Dewey's fleet on patrol, the Philippine rebels completed the defeat of the Spanish on land.

However, to the surprise of the Filipino people, the United States forces showed no signs of leaving. They soon learned that the Americans had come to stay, to begin a military occupation of their islands.

In time, the United States found itself fighting a nasty, three-year war against the native population. Betrayed in their struggle for independence, the islanders fought on in guerrilla fashion.

McKinley was deaf to their pleas for self-rule. Again and again he repeated that the Filipinos were "not ready" to govern themselves. Once more, it was the white man expressing an old belief—that he can run other people's lives better than they can themselves.

This was a time of corrupt politics in the United States, when hardly any major city could hold an honest election. The entire South had robbed the large black population of its voting rights. And yet Americans saw nothing strange in telling the Filipino people that they were incapable of choosing their own government.

Senator Henry Cabot Lodge listed for his colleagues why it was necessary for the United States to bring "peace and order" to the Philippines:

> From these islands comes now the best hemp in the world. Their forests are untouched, and with a variety of hardwoods of almost unexampled value.
>   Gold is found throughout the islands. . . . There are regions in Luzon containing great and valuable deposits of copper. But the chief mineral value of the islands is in their undeveloped coal beds.

The President had a homelier version of why his government refused to let go of the islands. "I walked the floor of the White House night after night," he told a group of clergymen, "and I am not ashamed to tell you, gentlemen, that I went down on my knees and prayed to Almighty God for light and guidance. And one night late, it came to me."

What came to President McKinley was the revelation that none of the Philippine Islands should be given to any other nation, nor should the people be left to govern themselves.

"There was nothing left for us to do but take them all," declared the President to the visiting ministers, "and to

educate the Filipinos, and uplift and civilize and Christian-
ize them."

From the Philippines came ugly reports that the American army was using barbarous methods in subduing the
island people. Civilians were slaughtered in great numbers.
Whole towns were put to the torch. Captives were subjected
to cruel tortures or killed outright.

"Our troops in the Philippines," wrote Henry Nelson
Loomis, correspondent of the *Boston Herald,* "look upon all
Filipinos as of one race and condition, and being dark men,
they are therefore 'niggers' and entitled to all the contempt and harsh treatment administered by white over-
lords to the most inferior races."

The year 1899 and the century ended with the spangled
banner flying over Hawaii, Cuba, Samoa, Puerto Rico,
Guam, and the Philippines. Some eight million additional
dark-skinned people had come under United States rule.
But hardly as equals. They were "little brown brothers," in
the then-current phrase. The administration in Washington
had no intention that they would be considered as full-
fledged citizens.

Some Americans noted how heedlessly this nation had
suddenly seized an empire. It was all a clear-cut matter of
science and natural law, as the President saw it. The relations between peoples were guided by "the doctrine of evolution and the rule of the survival of the fittest," McKinley
said. The new century would bring some new insights into
science and natural law.

THE NEW CENTURY
"Inequality Is a Law of Life"

"We are trustees of the world's progress . . . and what shall history say of us? Shall it say that, called to command the proudest, ablest, purest race of history, we declined?"

The speaker was a self-assured, fair-haired young senator from Indiana, who was frequently carried away with his own eloquence. Senator Albert J. Beveridge made his maiden speech after the New Year in 1900. Fired with patriotism, he cried out:

> God has not been preparing the English-speaking and Teutonic peoples for a thousand years for nothing. No! He has made us the master organizers of the world. . . . And of all of our race, He has marked the American people as His chosen nation to finally lead in the regeneration of the world.

America had awakened in the dawning century, cocksure and self-righteous as only a mighty nation can be. Amid the ringing bells of the New Year, leading spokesmen unloosed a torrent of appeals to blood, race, country. To Senator Beveridge, speaking in the Capitol, the duty to dominate the dark-skinned peoples of the world was "in our blood." And he uttered a pious hope to heaven that the easy life led by Americans had not "so debased our blood that we will fear to shed it for the flag and its imperial destiny."

Most white Americans of that era shared the opinion that white supremacy centered in the "blood." These were some of the popular beliefs: That the world's destiny flowed in the "red blood" of America's sons and daughters; that the sacred duty of parents was to pass on their "pure blood" to future generations; that most Americans, of whatever race, were "full-blooded," but others less fortunate were of "mixed blood"; that one drop of "inferior blood" was enough to bar a person from the white race. In some mysterious way, blood was believed to determine the quality of every person, the bond that drew together all those of the same racial strain.

In a high-towered university not far from the nation's capital, scientists peered through their microscopes. They looked in vain for a shred of truth in any of the commonly held beliefs about the "blood."

The biologists had verified the fact that a father contributes no blood whatever to his children. Nor was there any evidence that the blood of a mother freely intermixes with that of her unborn child. Moreover, the microscope revealed no "Negro blood" and no "white blood," no "mixed blood" and no "pure blood."

Strangely enough, it was the Old Testament that had stated the case with a good deal of accuracy: "God has made of one blood all the nations that dwell on the face of the earth."

However, it would take more than either the Bible or scientific evidence to upset the "blood" notions that ran like a dark, mystical current throughout white America. No portion or function of the human body was more burdened with fear and falsehood. Ancient superstitions about blood were linked with the modern myths about race.

From the earliest arrival of black slaves in America, efforts were made to prevent any intermarriage of the races. If slavery was to be built on blackness, mixed parentage was to be strictly avoided. Laws were passed to keep black and white sexually apart.

Even more effective than laws were the fears which

were carefully spread throughout America. It was whispered that "the mixing of blood" would bring on sickness and feeble-mindedness and would produce defective children. Although large numbers of healthy children were clearly seen as the offspring of mixed parentage, the myths were widely believed.

State laws defined a Negro as a person having at least "one-sixteenth part of black blood." The lawmakers never bothered to explain why similar portions of white ancestry failed to make a person white. If fifteen forebears were white and the sixteenth was black (a great-great-grandparent), then the person was judged to be a Negro. In many states, that individual was not permitted to marry a white person.

The "blood" myths and the "blood" laws remained unchallenged. What had become well known in the scientific laboratory somehow never found its way into the law courts.

In those first years of the twentieth century, the study of human blood did disclose that there are different types of blood. Investigators found that blood fell into definite categories. They were first classified as A, O, and B, with AB later added as a fourth variety. The types were based on how the blood cells of one group react with those of another when they are mixed in a blood transfusion.

All the various types of blood were found among members of all races. The researchers learned that these characteristics of blood could not be linked with a person's skin color.

Clearly, the blood was not the carrier of mankind's biological heritage. But how were hereditary traits passed from one generation to the next? And why were some children born snub-nosed or long-legged, color-blind or brown-skinned?

The Gene

A Century of Science, was the hopeful prediction for the 1900s. And how promising was its first decade!

These were the years of Albert Einstein's theory of relativity, and of the quantum theory in physics. Astronomers expounded bold new ideas on the origin of the solar system. And the air was filled with startling new sounds—the whir of dynamos, the crackle of wireless, the backfiring of automobiles.

In the stillness of the biology laboratory, the scientist found himself witnessing the process which begins new life. His interest was focused on the fusion of two cells, one from each parent. It was this fertilized egg which then divided itself again and again to form a new living being.

Inside the fertilized egg was the nucleus and a cluster of threadlike structures known as chromosomes. The probers were convinced that here lay the secret of human heredity.

Within each species, parents produced exactly their own kinds of offspring. Chromosomes held the key to every new being, each one unique. The pattern for a human baby was set out in the chromosomes handed down by its parents. And those few physical traits which placed a newborn child into one of the human races—these too were contained in the chromosomes.

With the beginning of the new century, several biologists, working separately, had come to similar conclusions about heredity. They also found some of these same ideas in a long-forgotten document—the writings of Gregor Mendel. In raising and crossing garden peas, the science-minded monk had discovered many of the principles of heredity.

Mendel crossed a tall plant with a short plant, finding that he produced nothing but tall plants. Had the tall parent canceled out shortness? Mendel thought the answer was yes—until a short plant appeared in the next generation.

The peculiar hide-and-seek of certain traits finally led Mendel straight to a new discovery: the offspring derived a corresponding unit for every inherited trait from each of its parents. But these units or factors were not always equal in their influence on the child's makeup. One of the two units might be a dominant type. Such a dominant unit would tend to assert itself in determining the physical trait of the offspring.

The other inherited unit might be recessive. It merely remained inactive, dormant. Hidden in one generation, it might reappear in the next, if coupled with a matching recessive unit. The patterns of inheritance, Mendel learned, worked out the same for all inborn traits.

Among his garden peas, the monk experimented with such factors as the color of the flower, the shape of seed and pod. And Mendel made one further important discovery. The individual traits of the parent plants were not blended in the offspring. In breeding a yellow-flowered pea plant with a green-flowered one, the new generations had either yellow or green flowers. Never were they a yellowish green or a greenish yellow. His experiments with garden peas showed that each inherited factor remained whole and separate, never mixed or combined.

In 1900 many scientists were raising peas. Mendel's experiments were being repeated and his conclusions put to rigorous testing. Some of the processes within the plant which were invisible to Mendel could now be seen under the improved microscope. The researchers checked not only the heredity of garden peas but also that of sea urchins, primroses, grasshoppers, fruit flies.

Before the end of the decade, Mendel's unit of heredity would have a name—the gene. And a new science, genetics, would eventually probe the patterns of heredity in human beings.

At the same time, men were suddenly seeking information not merely measured in grams, centimeters, or light years. An expanding age of science had extended its scope to the entire subject of mankind and all its works. The social sciences asked: How did men live? What were their goals and problems? How did they function as members of families, communities, nations, races? The search for truth was widening.

A View from Above

By 1905 the study of human societies had become a new feature on American college campuses. Students flocked to courses in sociology. At Yale, they studied what they called "Sumnerology." In class, they listened to the forceful and fixed opinions of William Graham Sumner. The crusty Professor Sumner didn't even like the word "sociology" and named his course "The Science of Society."

In those years, nearby New Haven and other Connecticut towns were filled with thousands of Italian immigrants, newly arrived and faced with many social problems. Across America, large foreign-born populations were being thrown into rivalry for jobs in the Pittsburgh mills, the Chicago stockyards, the mine and lumber camps in a dozen states. Women worked long hours in sweatshops, and small children toiled in the coal mines.

The South continued to be a dark, violent world where a black man could be tortured to death for the smallest offense—or for none at all. The problems of race in America had spread out nationwide. Negroes were steadily streaming northward and into the big cities. Here would come the next painful ordeal for a society that liked to picture itself as open and free. In the urban centers, America would test its own readiness for democracy. This was certainly a troubled society that could use help—from scientists or anyone else.

But the social science of William Graham Sumner was not meant to help. The Yale professor was strangely indifferent to everyday human problems. Society was to be studied as though from a treetop in some jungle, with the beasts below fighting out the principle of "the survival of the fittest."

Sumner looked like a bank president, with a trim mustache, a wing collar, and the tiny spectacles that he clipped to his nose. His classroom manner was cold and gruff, matching the stern dogma which he preached.

If the "unfit" are helped to survive, he argued, America's progress would suffer. Sumner had no sympathy for "tramps and outcasts, the poor and the weak, paupers and loafers, the ignorant and the illiterate." They deserved to be eliminated, he believed, while Nature "grants her rewards to the fittest." At the heart of Sumnerology was the idea of the natural superiority of some groups in society over others. And to Sumner it was clear that the superior breed had won out in America.

Sumner was a product of his age—and so was his social science. For more than a quarter of a century the professor dominated the social thinking at Yale and other universities across the land. He poured out hundreds of short essays, which found their way into the nation's leading newspapers and magazines. Sumner was an institution, a major influence in his time.

The Yale professor had caught sight of an important principle of social science—that the cultural influences or folkways of a society are important in shaping the behavior of its members. But Sumner failed to understand the extent to which folkways were themselves subject to change. He insisted that every culture was a rigid mold, resistant to new influences.

Although he had been trained as a clergyman, Sumner voiced the dominant attitudes of the day. For him, the suffering of the poor was a necessary price of progress. Greed was merely a part of the spirit of free competition. Racial bigotry was something built into the makeup of man. These were what Sumner called "folkways" or "mores." And because he supposed that they were founded on human nature, Sumner believed firmly that such practices could not be changed by legislation, education, or reform.

"Nothing is more certain than that inequality is a law of life," Sumner lectured. "If you asked Thomas Jefferson whether in 'All men are created equal' he meant to include Negroes, he would have said he was not talking about Negroes. Ask anyone who says it now whether he means to include foreigners—Russian Jews, Hungarians, Italians— he would draw his line somewhere."

Any effort to bring about equality in this country was simply a scheme "to rob A in order to give to B," Sumner charged. "All such plans nourish some of the meanest vices of human nature." The professor shook a warning forefinger at those who were engaged in "an absurd effort to make the world over."

If social science was one thing at Yale, it was quite another at Atlanta University. The small Georgia school, with an all-Negro student body, was becoming noted for its scientific studies of life in the South. The director of that program was W. E. B. Du Bois, now a handsome young scholar, prematurely bald, with a pointed beard.

Sumner's method was to preach his own gospel; Du Bois

emphasized truth-seeking, tireless research. Sumner remained locked within Yale's gothic towers; Du Bois and his students roamed the countryside, studying society in the places where people lived and worked.

At Yale social science was all theory, but Atlanta combined theory with action. Sumner was aghast at the thought of social change. Du Bois sought to alter a society that could produce such institutions as Jim Crow, lynching, and poverty based on race.

Social Scientist

In the year 1905 W. E. B. Du Bois was on his way across the state of Georgia toward his home and his family. Atlanta, where he lived, was a city wild with fire and bloodshed. After four days of rioting, the news had drifted down into the countryside where Du Bois had been collecting data from sharecroppers.

He first heard the report in a tiny church where a few families gathered to share their sorrow. Du Bois took the night train homeward. Valdosta to Tifton, and Cordele to Macon—the engine wailed at the crossings.

Sitting alone in the dingy coach, Du Bois wrote bits of prayerful verse, pouring out his feelings of anger and grief. "We bow our heads and hearken soft to the sobbing of women and children," he wrote. "We beseech Thee to hear us, good Lord!"

In Atlanta, Du Bois, tense and anxious, hastened to his family. The campus of the Negro university and the nearby black community showed the grim signs of the terror attacks. Homes of black people were burned to the ground, some still smoldering. Five Negroes were dead. Many were beaten by the mobs.

Though a distinguished scholar, in moments like this Du Bois was filled with dismay and with self-doubt as well.

Could he remain the placid college professor in such an age? What was the value of rationality when innocent men were being made the victims of madness?

His educational background had trained him to be a social scientist. And throughout his lifetime, Du Bois remained committed to the idea that "the careful reasoning of the human mind, backed by the facts of science, is the one salvation of man." But he had seen science too often put to the uses of race hatred.

At Atlanta, Du Bois planned and directed a series of studies which were hailed as a pioneer effort in the scientific investigation of social conditions. For ten years the series of Atlanta Studies came out yearly, each one a thorough and masterful piece of research on some aspect of Negro life—population, family life, health, business opportunities, education.

No one before him had ever attempted such studies. Du Bois was trying to take his first steps in sociology "as the science of human action." For him, the knowledge obtained through field research was a necessary means for bringing about a change.

Slight of build, wearing city clothes, Du Bois could be found in the Georgia back country, making his way from cabin to one-roomed cabin. Tirelessly, he posed his questions and recorded his facts.

"What rent do you pay?" A shrug and a sigh, and then the answer, "All we make."

"But what happens when you work harder and have a good crop?"

"The rent goes up."

In an abandoned barn, a dozen dark-skinned children of widely assorted ages sat on logs. In such unlikely schoolhouses as this, Negroes in the South had managed to cut illiteracy in half in the period since slavery days.

Du Bois's probing led him to a foul-smelling backwoods distillery, where turpentine was extracted from pine sap. The entire work force was made up of black convicts, serving time and "loaned" to the factory owner on contract. Across the South, thousands of chained prisoners worked railroads, plantations, mines.

"Only the colored are sent to jail," Du Bois was told, "and not because they are guilty. The state needs convicts to hire out in forced labor."

From his accumulated facts emerged a precise picture of Negro life. Du Bois wrote his own rich accounts of what he saw, bringing to life the dry statistics and records. "It is easy for us to lose ourselves in details," he wrote. "We often forget that each unit in the mass is a throbbing human soul."

He was a dignified man, who sometimes seemed aloof and detached. But actually, Du Bois was keenly sensitive to the whiplash of race hatred wherever it touched any black man or woman. Each lynching opened a wound that left him with a scar.

In the southern countryside, the northern-born, college-educated Du Bois found himself at home. Here he ripened in the bosom of black folk, lost his academic stuffiness, discovered his deep love for his own people, came to know the true condition of their existence.

He grieved over the miseducation of both black and white children, robbed of an understanding of the role that all races play in the advancement of mankind. "How easy, by emphasis and omission, to make children believe that every great soul the world ever saw was a white man's soul," he wrote, "that every great thought the world ever knew was a white man's thought; that every great deed was a white man's deed."

In the year 1906, Du Bois brought a friend to speak at the Atlanta University commencement exercises. The speaker was a white man, short and slender, who spoke in a German accent and revealed an immense knowledge of the culture of Africa. Professor Franz Boas of Columbia University was a distinguished anthropologist.

White Southerners had a habit of repeating that they alone knew "the nigra and what's good for him." Boas pointed out that the white Southerner could see black men and women only from "a narrow field of experience," and actually knew little about this whole people, their background, their capabilities. The visiting professor outlined the vast heritage of the Negro in the African civilizations that discovered iron-working, built great cities, created a rich treasury of art masterpieces, devised remarkable systems of law courts. Boas urged that the Atlanta students help to reclaim this cultural legacy, to recover for the Negro people "the strength that was their own before they set foot on the shores of this continent."

For Du Bois, the words of Boas were fresh encouragement for a large work he had undertaken—the writing of a giant encyclopedia of Africana. Clearly, Du Bois saw the Negro-American in his kinship with dark-skinned people the world over, part of the great majority of mankind.

Mainly he took deep pride in the Negro masses of the United States, then nearly ten million in number. He observed new generations of black men and women, utterly changed from those who had come out of the confining mold of slavery. He discovered the vein of high courage that ran among them—even at a time when the Negro's fortunes in America had sunk low. To his students he spoke with hope, denying vigorously that they were doomed to lead lives as servants and menial laborers.

Du Bois unloosed his anger against the Negro leader Booker T. Washington as a man who "accepts the alleged inferiority of the Negro race." Washington was an outstanding builder of Negro schools. His aim was a limited and practical one. Washington's schools were designed to prepare black students to take their places as workers on the farm and in the factory. In this way, he thought, blacks would realize a sense of independence and self-worth.

Washington was trying to "take the eyes of these millions off the stars," Du Bois charged scornfully, "and if they dream dreams, let them be dreams of corn bread and molasses."

In the late spring of 1909, Du Bois was in New York City. A seedbed of action which he had helped to plant was beginning to blossom. Months of patient work had produced a meeting of black and white leaders ready to deal with problems of race relations.

More than two hundred persons had gathered for several days of earnest preparation for activity to win civil rights and educational and employment opportunities for black America. Out of that conference came the National Association for the Advancement of Colored People.

The conference began with what Du Bois saw as "the very points around which the real race argument centers today: from the standpoint of science, are Negroes men?" From a panel of scientists who were present came the sober response that the notion of black inferiority was wholly without any factual basis.

Anthropologists had begun to throw a strong scientific light on the murky subject of human races. The studies of Franz Boas outshone all the rest.

A TIME OF TRIAL
"A World Safe for Democracy"

Franz Boas learned of bigotry first-hand in the little German town of Minden where he was raised. His was one of the two Jewish families in the town.

Hate-filled attacks left their marks on his thinking. Even more visible were several facial scars. Often, a Jewish student at the university was compelled to fight a saber duel as an answer to an anti-Semitic attack. Germany was then a nation displaying the anti-Jewish hatreds which would later run riot in the Nazi period.

A sensitive boy and a brilliant student, young Franz Boas found his deepest interests in nature study and music. His family encouraged the free flow of opinions, and Franz grew up with a fierce devotion to democratic ideas.

In 1883, as a student on a scientific expedition, the young man traveled by dog sled with a few Eskimo companions far beyond the Arctic Circle. His year on Baffin Island changed the direction of his life. He became, as he said, "an Eskimo among Eskimos." He was fascinated by these people and their way of life. Boas arrived in the Arctic as a mapmaker and geographer. When he left his Eskimo companions, he was ready for a lifelong career in anthropology.

Franz said goodbye to his Arctic friends with sorrow. "I had seen that they enjoyed life—and a hard life—as we do," he told his family, "that nature is also beautiful to them; that feelings of friendship also root in the Eskimo heart. Although the character of their life is so rude as compared to civilized life, the Eskimo is a man as we are."

Boas was to return many times to the Eskimos, and to spend much of his life among Indians and remote peoples. He had begun a lifelong search to answer the question, "What determines the behavior of human societies?"

He realized with a shock that his first answers to that question were wrong. He had discovered that although people inherit certain traits from their parents, this endowment cannot, by itself, explain the kinds of social lives they live. He went to the Arctic with the idea that perhaps it was geography—the physical surroundings—that controlled life patterns. But he could see that even the harsh conditions of the frozen north could not wholly account for the social traditions of the Eskimo people.

Boas carried his field work into new areas of anthropological study. In 1886 he began a program of research among the Kwakiutl Indians far up the Pacific coast of North America. These tribes had had only bad experiences with white people—traders, missionaries, and government agents. Boas had a hard time persuading them that he was none of these.

To explain his mission he gathered the Indians and made a little speech: "My people live far away and would like to know what people in distant lands do. And they said to me, 'Go and see what the people in this land do.' And so I came here and I saw you eat and drink, sing and dance. And I shall go back and say, 'This is how the people there live.'"

Boas learned the languages of the natives wherever he went—even though he spoke them all with a German accent. As a master linguist he was able to report that there are no inferior languages, just as there are no inferior cultures. He found languages rich in those words and phrases that have special significance to the peoples who speak them. For example, English has only one word for snow;

but the Eskimos have many, depending on whether they are talking about snow on the ground, falling snow, drifting snow, or snow in a snowdrift.

Continuing his tireless work in the field, Boas began teaching at Columbia University, where he remained for forty-six years. He was a small, wiry man, with piercing black eyes, a high forehead, and an unruly crop of hair. Boas was loved by his students, a great many of whom became outstanding anthropologists. He built a great reputation for his university as a center for the study of the science of man and his works.

He also became curator at the American Museum of Natural History. Boas's worldwide expeditions brought back important treasures of anthropological data. One study traced the origins of the native American peoples to Asia. His students searched for the links between Siberians and those wanderers who crossed a land bridge that existed thousands of years ago. Were these the ancestors of the Eskimo and American Indian populations?

At the turn of the century, Boas's busy life centered on Columbia University, near the Hudson River in uptown New York. Each day, Boas rode the Hudson ferry to his home on the New Jersey side, where he lived with his family. Not far from Columbia was the American Museum of Natural History, where Boas made the science of anthropology more understandable in graphic exhibits for the public.

With Boas, anthropology crossed a great divide into the new century. This science had formerly served some of the most backward popular beliefs about mankind. The words of anthropologists were used throughout the nineteenth century to justify slavery, support race hatred, and build the false structure of white supremacy.

Boas's book, *The Mind of Primitive Man,* was a major scientific work that systematically disproved the doctrine of the "super-race." One by one, Boas took the most commonly held beliefs about white supremacy and showed that they held not a shred of truth.

But bigotry in America had always been deep-planted and well fortified. It would survive many a powerful assault by fact and reason. Boas had struck a blow for truth and equality. The counterattack was not long in coming.

A Dangerous Dictionary

In the year 1910, the riddle of race was officially declared solved.

The United States Immigration Commission proudly presented its *Dictionary of Races,* on which some three hundred government employees had labored for three years. Supposedly, the troublesome problem of races was neatly entrapped between the covers of the massive *Dictionary,* somewhere within its forty-two volumes.

More than a million immigrants were arriving in the United States that year. People with dark skins, unfamiliar languages and customs were pouring in at a steady rate. Many American-born whites had begun to growl about the inflow. There was much grumbling about what was happening to "the pure American stock." This country, it was said, could possibly be committing "race suicide."

The government in Washington was not ready to close the gates on the foreign born. But the *Dictionary of Races* was its effort to classify people into neat racial groups so that a label could be pinned on every new arrival, as well as on those who were already here.

Without any scientific basis, many ethnic groups were

officially classified as separate races. Referring to the Jews, the *Dictionary* said, "Physically the Hebrew is a mixed race, like all our immigrant races or peoples, although to a less degree than most." Another example of unclarity and error was the classifying of a number of dark-skinned people from Southeast Asia and the Pacific islands as "Negroes." "They are alike in inhabiting hot countries and in belonging to the lowest division of mankind from an evolutionary standpoint."

The government publication not only drew hundreds of sharp racial lines, but also described people such as the southern Italians as "excitable, impulsive, highly imaginative, impracticable," and the northern Italians as "cool, deliberate, patient, practical." The book added that those from southern Italy are given to "crimes, and especially violent crimes."

In describing the Japanese, the *Dictionary* referred to a "coarse" type and a "fine" type. The latter, it was pointed out, has an admixture of the "Caucasian-like" Ainu strain. Serbo-Croatians were said to have "savage manners." Poles were "high-strung." The people from eastern and southern Europe were characterized as being "different in temperament and civilization from ourselves."

Some of the writers of the *Dictionary* were well-known scientists. However, one eminent anthropologist who had been involved for a short time angrily condemned the whole project. For Franz Boas, the *Dictionary* was one more attempt to relegate racial types to fixed pigeonholes and to rank them in quality.

Before the government document was published, Boas was already hard at work on his own book dealing with the science of peoples and races. His ideas had been fitting themselves together in his mind for twenty-five years.

The Mold of Culture

At Columbia University Boas kept in close touch with the new developments in biology.

In those early years of the century, the study of genetics was tracing the flow of genes from parent to offspring, certain traits repeating themselves in successive generations. For Boas, however, the scientific problem was to place into balance the mixture of the many influences that were at work on human beings and on human societies.

Race might explain certain physical differences between groups of people. But race did not determine the functioning of their minds. And people could not be placed into racial categories simply by observing their behavior, customs, languages.

Boas ranged widely as a keen observer of human societies, from the coastal villages of British Columbia to the ethnic ghettoes of big American cities, from the island cultures of the Caribbean to the tribal cultures of the American Southwest. His laboratory became the entire North American continent. Wherever he studied man and his societies, Boas learned that there was little about the nature of any people or race that could be reduced to a simple dictionary definition.

As individuals, human beings varied greatly from person to person. As societies, men lived by certain changing cultural patterns. As races, groups of people held a few physical traits in common. As a species, mankind was one, differing fundamentally from all other species, not only in appearance but in the quality of the mind. As Boas put it, "the functions of the human mind are common to the whole of humanity."

Even in the simplest societies, the anthropologist revealed, "no tribe has ever been found that does not possess a well-organized language; no community that does not know the use of instruments for breaking, cutting, or drilling, the use of fire and of weapons with which to defend themselves and to obtain the means of living."

Anthropologists like Boas and his students pioneered in studies of such cultural patterns as the mating rituals of Navahos, the street games of urban children, seal hunting among Eskimos, the music of black people.

Boas suggested that the truth about a people's behavior and life style was not to be found simply in their genes, their "blood," their race. Instead he called attention to "the external and social causes which have molded the characters of people."

A complex range of influences follows every person through life. The birth day of a human being brings not a single gift. Each new arrival receives a threefold heritage —genes, environment, culture. Of the three, however, only the genetic inheritance is already fixed at birth. The other endowments begin at birth and function in changing patterns all through life.

In every society, its members live by certain accepted styles of behavior. These are not fixed for all time. Every generation adds something new to the characteristics of societies. Such cultural traits as skills, languages, morals, institutions, arts, traditions are learned, shared, passed on from one generation to the next.

"These qualities," said Boas, "are the result of social conditions rather than hereditary traits."

A wide variety of life styles has appeared among mankind. But in America, Boas pointed out, different ways of living were often seen by white observers through the veil of their own prejudices. To men frantically building an industrial society, those who lived closer to the patterns of nature might appear as "backward." Strangely, such people might even be considered "unfit" to survive—or without the right to live their own way.

"Living Fossil"

On a March day in the year 1916, an Indian died in a San Francisco museum. The death of "Ishi" marked the end of the Yahi people, a tribe of California Indians.

"Ishi" was not his real name. He would not reveal his name to white people, whom he called *saltu*, a word in his own language meaning beings of another order, nonhumans.

The tragedy of Ishi's people, who once numbered in the thousands, was that they did not die out from natural causes. Between 1844, when California became a United States possession, and the time of Ishi's death, the Yahis were purposely hunted down and exterminated. This was a people who led a simple life. They never acquired riding horses or firearms.

Ishi was born about the time of the Civil War. From his earliest childhood, he and his family knew only the life of fugitives. His people were pursued by bands of white settlers, self-appointed troops of vigilantes, and the army. A series of raids against the tribe steadily reduced their numbers. In 1871 a large number of Yahi men, women, and children were trapped in a cave and massacred.

From that time on, the child Ishi lived in hiding, with the remaining Yahis, amid the northern peaks of the Sierra Nevada. By 1911 Ishi was a lone survivor. Crazed with loneliness, he surrendered, resigned to a terrible fate among "the white savages" who had destroyed his people.

Ishi's next five years were spent at the University of California. Anthropologists were able to piece together some Yahi language. The wild Indian turned out to be a pleasant but shy, dignified man. He represented an ancient and simple style of living in a land which had been the home of his people for thousands of years. Although he was pictured in the newspapers as a "living fossil," Ishi came out of a culture which perhaps had much to teach the white man about how to live with his natural environment. That culture disappeared completely in 1916. Ishi lived out his last days in an unused exhibit hall of the museum, which was converted into living quarters. Anthropologists arranged for proper medical care and hoped the ailing man would get plenty of air and sunlight. He died of a "white man's disease"—tuberculosis.

The grim story of the Yahis was pieced together from many documents and reports, letters and diaries. A sheriff had written a journal which recorded his part in many of the most devastating attacks on the doomed tribe. He told of riding with his party on one Indian camp—but the death scene they found showed that other white raiders had already been there. "There was not a bad Indian to be found," the sheriff wrote. "But about forty good ones lay scattered about."

The pioneeers who settled America shut out of their thinking any idea that the Indian might have rights to the land or that its natural bounty might be shared with him. Race hatred was an easier turn of mind. It suited white Americans to picture the Indian as a "savage," pagan, violent, and backward.

President Theodore Roosevelt voiced the more "liberal" view of the day: "I don't go so far as to think that the only good Indians are dead Indians, but I believe that nine out of ten are, and I shouldn't inquire too closely into the case of the tenth."

The story of Ishi and the Yahis underscored a disturbing truth. If a whole people is defined as inferior, that nation or population or race may be doomed to death. The Yahis numbered only a few thousand. But before many decades passed, the world would see race hatred destroying millions of "inferior" people.

To Franz Boas, there was something revolting about the notion of peoples being judged and graded, approved and disapproved—as though they were animals in the stockyards. Most distressing to the Columbia professor was the realization that such attitudes had the blessings of "science."

Anthropologists of the past had helped to work out a theory of cultural evolution that gave support to current notions about races and peoples. This once again was a distortion of Darwin's ideas about evolution. The doctrine of cultural evolution attempted to show that all societies could be rated according to various levels of "savagery," "barbarism," and "civilization." The theory was that all peoples had to pass through the same series of stages on their way to the top.

The dogma was a comfortable one for the twentieth-century white American. According to this view, he had reached the pinnacle of human striving. From his august heights, he could look down on other peoples and decide which of the lower stages each group was in. As a member of a "super" nation and a "super" race, he might even decide the fate of "inferior" peoples.

These doctrines clashed sharply with everything that Boas and other scientists were discovering about human societies. Various peoples lived differently. Each might have its own path of development. But all were entitled to their own life style as long as there was no interference with the rights of others.

Boas had observed closely the life of a Polynesian island, a Swiss town, an African village, a Chinese city, an Indian tribe, an American urban community. Who could judge which represented the superior culture? For Boas, there was no hierarchy of cultures. He rejected "one single general line of development" as the course for all mankind. "There may be other civilizations," he wrote, "based perhaps on different traditions and on different equilibrium of emotion and reason which are of no less value than our own."

A few voices in those years had begun to question whether America really had nothing to learn from other cultures. Here, an industrial order had created a nation of rich people getting richer and of poor people getting poorer; the natural environment of America was being rapidly devastated; and every eighth person, dark-skinned, was being denied his civil rights.

Moreover, the most "highly civilized" nations of the world—the United States included—were just then preparing to sacrifice millions of human lives in the first of the World Wars.

Tests and Truth

Suddenly the United States was a nation in the throes of World War I, and five million of its men would be bearing arms before it was over. In the summer of 1917 Americans were saving scrap paper, buying Liberty Bonds, singing "Over There."

With war declared, hatreds were set loose across the nation. Antiwar dissenters of all kinds were dealt with harshly. Violence flared in the cities between people of different ethnic backgrounds. Black men who answered the call to the military service and war industry were attacked by mobs. In a war supposedly being fought for democracy, it was democracy that became the first casualty.

At army camps, drafted men not only struggled with the mastery of an unfamiliar and unaccustomed way of life but also had to contend with something quite new—the army intelligence tests. Psychologists had devised a series of questions and answers which were given to almost two million soldiers.

The tests proved to be useful in some ways: for discharging from the army some men suffering from serious mental illness; in measuring the problems of illiteracy; in helping select men suited for officer training.

However, the testers took on an additional task for which there was no reasonable basis. They used the test scores in an effort to compare the innate intelligence of soldiers by national origin or by race.

Tests of this kind were invented years before by a Frenchman named Alfred Binet. While he believed in their usefulness for certain purposes in the educational system, Binet made it clear that the tests had certain built-in shortcomings. The inborn intelligence of two groups of people could be compared, he said, but only if the two groups had lived their lives in identical cultural backgrounds.

Binet's warning was completely lost on the army testers. It was as though they were trying to prove something—and they did. Or so they claimed when they made their reports.

Many years later, it was shown that the army tests were poorly designed and even "loaded" to bring about certain results. One expert admitted that some questions were designed to get what he called a "typically American" answer

—and anyone who failed to give such an answer was "un-desirable."

One type of question went like this: "Why are criminals locked up?" The soldier taking the test was to check one of three answers: "to protect society"; "to get even with them"; "to make them work." Clearly, the answer given would depend on one's own experiences with law enforcement.

To some extent, the answers might show what a person's behavior would be in a given situation. But in no sense did they measure the intelligence with which an individual was born—nor could they indicate the intelligence of a whole race!

Further, the testers had no definitive standards for classifying men as "Negro" or "white." No effort was even made to determine the true ancestry of those taking the tests.

With a loud fanfare of publicity, the army announced that the average of the scores made by Negroes was below the average made by the whites. Colonel Robert M. Yerkes, in charge of the army experiment, added his opinion that the tests "brought into clear relief the intellectual inferiority of the Negro."

His associate, Dr. Carl C. Brigham, echoed those conclusions. It was not until ten years later that Brigham changed his mind. He admitted that such tests could not compare the intelligence of racial or national groups, that the summary which he had made was "without foundation."

But it was clear that white supremacy had fashioned for itself another deadly weapon. Similar "intelligence tests" would be used again and again in an effort to drive black people down. In fact, such false "scientific" methods would be reused whenever black people appeared to be making some gains against the forces of bigotry.

Meanwhile World War I had brought thousands of black

people streaming into the industrial centers of America, where they were working in skilled jobs at improved earnings. One of the most outspoken racists in the United States Senate was Mississippi's James K. Vardaman, who felt that "horrible problems" would grow out of the wartime advances which black people had made. "Impress the Negro with the fact that he is defending the flag," warned Vardaman, "teach him it is his duty to keep the emblem of the Nation flying—it is but a short step to the conclusion that his political rights must be respected."

But "the war to make the world safe for democracy" had barely ended before Negroes felt a new wave of repressive terror. Both in the North and the South, black war veterans were lynched while they were still in their service uniforms. On Chicago's South Side, the skies flared red in five days of anti-Negro rioting, arson, and violence which took thirty-eight lives.

The Twenties were to open with hooded Klansmen marching in the main streets of American cities throughout the land.

THE NINETEEN TWENTIES
"Whose Country Is This?"

The spring that spread across America in 1920 brought not only blossoms and birdsong but also the Ku Klux Klan, parading in deathly silence through hundreds of towns.

The hooded marchers were not merely ghosts out of the past. The new KKK expanded from its base in the South into every state. Still anti-Negro, the revived KKK widened its message of hatred to include the foreign born, Catholics, Jews, and Orientals. It had now become a flag-waving "patriotic" order, rapidly reaching a nationwide membership of four million.

In wild growth, bigotry that season took many forms. By May, Henry Ford, the nation's leading industrialist, launched a propaganda campaign against Jews. His local automobile agencies began pouring tons of hate literature into thousands of American communities.

That same spring, California passed a new law prohibiting the Japanese from owning land. Alabama adopted legislation aimed against Catholics. In "Bloody Williamson County," Illinois, violence flared against Italian coal miners. The government recorded twenty major anti-Negro race riots in a single year.

In the name of pure-blooded one hundred percent Americanism a fanatical wave of hate and fear swept across the land. At the core of America's bigotry was the old belief in the inferiority of the Negro. But the fever spread rapidly in those years against any group that might be considered alien or different or strange.

The "race" now favored in this country was variously

called Anglo-Saxon, Teutonic, Aryan, Nordic. A white skin was no longer the badge of full membership in the "master race."

In their fevered nightmares, men seemed to see a "Catholic conspiracy"—or else it was the menace of "the International Jew." Broken English or a swarthy complexion were supposed to be tell-tale marks of an "inferior" breed.

A series of standardized types was pieced together, supposedly representing each of the despised groups—the belligerent Irishman, the shiftless Negro, the savage Indian, the shrewd Jew, the untrustworthy Oriental, the evil Italian, the indolent Mexican. The movies, the radio, and comic strips were soon stamping these stereotypes on the minds of Americans, children included.

A social scientist tested school children with the following question: "Aladdin was the son of a poor tailor. He lived in Peking, the capital city of China. He was always lazy and liked to play better than to work. What kind of boy was he: Indian, Negro, Chinese, French or Dutch?" To the amazement of the researcher, most children failed to answer that Aladdin was Chinese. A link between the words "lazy" and "Negro" had become deeply etched into their minds.

Many of the stereotypes were self-contradictory. The Irishman was supposedly dull-witted, but also cunning in politics; the Italian was "dirty and repulsive," but also possessed of sinister charms. The Jew was a "capitalist" but also a radical anti-capitalist. The Negro was lazy, but he also worked at back-breaking jobs that others shunned.

If a white Anglo-Saxon achieved wealth, he was considered "wise and industrious"; but if a non–Anglo-Saxon person made similar gains, he was "crafty" and "greedy."

Stereotypes became a thoughtless pattern for making harsh judgments about a whole people, without seeing individual differences. This was a way of prejudging a person without knowing him. At the core of such blind prejudice was the notion that each individual behaves according to a set of inborn traits peculiar to certain groups.

If men were poor or jobless, badly nourished or in ill health, it was all a matter of "race." If some were rug peddlers, coal heavers, moneylenders, politicians, restaurant owners—that too was in their "blood." The high crime rate could be attributed to certain races, according to the current popular beliefs. Where fear kept some ethnic groups in their own small communities, it was considered "proof" of inborn, un-American traits. If some people did not speak English—they were obviously "inferior!"

Melting Pot?

To those who hoped that America had been outgrowing its bigotry, the 1920s delivered a warning shock. Suddenly it seemed as if the nation had learned nothing from its experience, science, or common sense.

This country was a home for many and varied individuals and groups. Each group had made a contribution. Science had proved that mankind was one, that pure races were a fallacy, that skin color had little significance. In the continuing research on the question of race, important new truths had emerged.

But feelings were running wild and deep across this land. The nation had come out of the fever of war into a panic-filled period of unemployment and insecurity. Men were thrown into mad rivalry for jobs, for a secure place in society. In this hate-charged scene, dark-skinned people, the foreign born, those with "un-American" political or religious beliefs were branded as outsiders.

In those years, some people liked to speak of America as

a melting pot. They saw the hundreds of racial and ethnic groups being thrown together into one giant cauldron of unity. Supposedly they were to mix and merge—until all were one. But that's not the way it was.

Across the nation, bigots responded to the cry of "America for Americans." Others fell into step behind the Ku Klux Klan banners demanding "the rights of the white race." The hatemongers swept state and local elections in the 1920s. And the old dogmas of white supremacy even made a comeback in the halls of learning.

In the Name of Science

Under the broad roof of the American Museum of Natural History two points of view came into sharp conflict. This institution had become renowned for its studies in anthropology, and Dr. Franz Boas had over many years done some of his finest work there. His students were among the museum's noted anthropologists.

Located on the rim of Central Park, this museum—the largest of its kind in the world—housed outstanding exhibits. Hundreds of scientists were busy on research projects in its behind-the-scenes laboratories, developing the newest ideas in the science of man.

However, the office of president was occupied by Henry Fairfield Osborn. His close friend, Madison Grant, was a trustee of the museum. The two shared some ideas about race that set scientific progress reeling backward.

Osborn argued that Negroes were of a separate species, with an intelligence lower than that of *Homo sapiens*. He championed a movement to preserve the "purity" of a select portion of the white race by strict control of mating and reproduction.

A dabbler in science, Madison Grant was a wealthy bachelor who detested American democracy. He believed firmly that only members of his class and race should be permitted to rule. To the snobbish Mr. Grant, the threat inherent in democracy was "the transfer of power from the higher to the lower races."

Grant and Osborn were not content merely with white supremacy. The theory on which they operated divided white people into three groups, depending on their European origins. Europe was split east to west into three "layers of races." The "lowest" were those people who lived along the shores of the Mediterranean. An intermediate race was called "Alpine." The top layer consisted of the Nordics. Any member of this latter group, according to Grant, was "the white man *par excellence.*"

Grant interpreted world history to suit this view. The greatest men of all time were Nordics, he said. Although he failed in his effort to classify Jesus Christ as a Nordic, he attributed the glories of classical Greece and Rome, the Italian Renaissance, and the Age of Discovery to the descendants of Nordic invaders who swept across Europe. Dante, Michelangelo, Leonardo da Vinci—such great figures could only have been migrant Nordics in Grant's view. The fall of great civilizations, he said, was due to the mixing of pure Nordic blood with the blood of inferior races.

The autocrat mourned the contamination of the blood of America's founders, all of whom he classified as Nordics. His book, which sold widely in the early 1920s, was called *The Passing of the Great Race.*

Black people were beneath Grant's contempt. He saw them as "willing followers who ask only to obey and to further the ideals and wishes of the master race." The only possible solution for Negroes, he said, was to confine them in large colonies from which they would be released each day to be used as laborers and servants.

Boas replied to the claims of Grant and Osborn with a biting article in the *New York Times* entitled, "Lo, the Poor Nordic!" Other scientists at the American Museum of Natural History joined in opposing the theory of Nordic superiority, showing it contained no truth.

However, Grant was not generally considered a fool or a fanatic. In the 1920s, his ideas had wide public acceptance, and he was respected as an anthropologist connected with one of America's greatest scientific institutions. Of his book, the magazine *Science* said that it was "a work of solid merit." Undoubtedly his writing added fuel to the race hatreds of the time. He boasted that his was a major influence in the passage by Congress of laws restricting immigration on the basis of race and national origin.

In February 1921 came the judgment of the administration in Washington. Calvin Coolidge, Vice-President of the United States, and soon to be President, wrote an article entitled "Whose Country Is This?" for the popular magazine *Good Housekeeping.*

Coolidge declared that in choosing who could live in this land, "racial considerations were too grave to be brushed aside."

"Biological laws tell us that certain people will not mix or blend," Coolidge wrote, adding that only the "Nordics propagate themselves successfully." This was the old race dogma, once again relying strongly on "science."

Also couching his theories in "scientific" language, Grant claimed that nature favors the "super-race," that is, the Nordics. This was again a twisting of Darwin's fitness theory to suit the purposes of white supremacy.

Grant added a crude distortion of Mendel's theory of

heredity as well. In Grant's warped interpretation, the character of each individual is fixed at birth. Every member of an "inferior" race is condemned to a life of "inferiority," was Grant's message. He hardly needed to add: for this lower order of beings, why bother with education, an improved social environment, or wider opportunities?

America at that moment was in the grip of another dogma, which viewed so-called racial traits as supposedly unchanging and final, permanent and paramount. In 1923, some of these "scientific" opinions were to undergo a test in a California court.

In the San Joaquin Valley of central California lived a large group of Armenian grape growers. Their origins were in a part of the Old World torn by ancient conflicts between east and west.

The state of California had adopted a law which prohibited Orientals from owning land. And an effort was being made to deprive the Armenians of their vineyards. Although old Armenia was in the Caucasus, the Armenian people were not Caucasians, according to the lawsuit. It was charged that Armenians were "round-headed," and this was considered proof that they were of the Mongoloid or Oriental race.

The defense attorneys reached Dr. Franz Boas. And the anthropologist made a study of two large groups of Armenians, those born in the old country and those born here. Measurements of their heads showed some startling differences. The foreign-born Armenians did tend toward head forms which were more rounded, as viewed from above. However, the American-born were more oval- or long-headed.

Dr. Boas revealed to the court some of the reasons. In the old country, Armenian babies were tightly swaddled on cradle boards, lying on their backs. In this position, the weight of the head tended to compress the bone structure of the skull so as to bring about greater "roundness." In America, the Armenian custom changed so that infants were free to move about—resulting in a natural "long-headedness." The suit against the Armenians was dismissed.

Dr. Boas was not only gratified in seeing justice done. For him, the case provided an opportunity to illustrate that many racial traits are not fixed nor can they be clearly defined. Further, his study revealed that even certain physical traits that are generally considered to be hereditary may be subject to change under given social conditions.

By the 1920s, the life sciences had produced some important new insights. Slowly, research was putting together the interlocking pieces of the puzzle describing how human heredity really works.

In the fertilized egg cell where each human life begins is the set of genes that affects the development of the individual. Scientists showed clearly that genes are particles of living matter that carry instructions. Genes keep the pattern of future growth within a limited range of possibilities. But the environment of each child will help shape the specific individual that develops.

What passes from parents to child is not blood type O or brown eyes, but instructions for such traits. The child's environment will have little or no effect on such genetic factors as these. However, height or baldness may be greatly influenced by the conditions of a person's life. As for musical talent, the genes may favor such paths of development—but only if the opportunities occur for realizing the inborn potential.

A great many genes carry a complete formula for the

making of a human being. These genes relate only to human biological characteristics that appear throughout the species. They determine human form and features, provide for the correct number of fingers, insure the human breathing apparatus, offer the recipe for warm, red blood.

The differences in genes give each person the starting point toward his own individuality. Where some few genes are shared by a large number of people with common ancestry, these may form the basis for a race.

As the 1920s ended, it was already clear to the students of genetics that skin color is determined not by one gene but by several. And these linked genes, coming from either parent, might each be recessive or dominant. Special traits typical of one race appear at times among all races—for example, kinky hair, a broad nose, the special kind of eyelid associated with Mongoloids. And yet, it was obvious that groups of people could be recognized as members of a race on the basis of their general appearance.

Scientists looked in vain, however, for evidence that race establishes a person's outlook or morals any more than it determines his skills or language. No particular personality or character traits appear exclusively among the members of any one race.

Students of race showed that the behavior patterns of a social group could be explained more by its history and its social status than by its genes. Cultural differences were a result of social processes—and a people could change its entire life style by a shift in its surrounding conditions.

"All races possess the ability to participate in a modern, democratic society," Boas pointed out. In order to be equal in such a society, people did not need to be identical or even similar in makeup. "If we were to select that most intelligent, imaginative, energetic and emotionally stable one-third of mankind," the anthropologist added, "all races would be represented."

At Columbia University, Dr. Boas, aging rapidly and in declining health, urged his students on. He realized that the young science of anthropology had much to learn—and a lot to unlearn as well.

CRISIS YEARS
"The Whole World Is Aflame"

In less than a century, American anthropology had built for itself a rambling scientific structure, with a few rickety annexes.

The chief builders were amateurs. With more book work than field work, relying more on probability than on proof, they constructed the new science of man. It covered such sprawling fields of knowledge as human origins, the fossil remains of ancient man, early and modern cultures and languages, societies and races.

In its founding days, anthropology borrowed generously from the reports of sailors and missionaries, traders and tourists. A few of the more energetic probers pulled themselves away from their libraries to dig in ancient ruins and to live among remote peoples. But early anthropology as a whole had never been strong on field work. Few conclusions and principles of the new science were based on firsthand research. And nowhere did anthropology prove to be more shaky than in its first conclusions about race.

During the entire nineteenth century, there was no American anthropologist who avoided the pitfalls of race prejudice. Some devoted themselves zealously to supporting the doctrines of white supremacy. Well into the twentieth century, leading anthropologists continued to erect new theories to glorify the "master race."

It was Franz Boas who called a halt. Small in size, Boas became a towering influence in anthropology. He vigorously opposed the piling of new and unfounded generalities on top of unverified facts. Instead, Boas emphasized painstaking research, truth-seeking field work.

Through the sheer force of his ideas and his personal example, social and cultural anthropology entered a fruitful era of fact-finding. He coached his own students in field work, saw to it that they secured funds for research expeditions. And he warned them to put more facts and fewer sweeping judgments into their reports.

As the 1930s began, Boas was in his seventies, fatigued, racked by illness, bowed in grief by the tragic death of his wife in an automobile accident. But it was no time to stop. The anthropologist was once again on his way to the home of the Indians of the far Northwest. When he returned, his long-awaited rest had to be postponed.

Race hatred was once more running riot, threatening human lives. This time the danger was worldwide, and the source was his native Germany.

Racism Rampant

Toward nightfall the square in front of Kiel University burst into flames. A large, frenzied crowd ringed the huge bonfire on a May night in 1933. The Nazis had taken power in Germany, and fire, terror, and bloodshed were spreading swiftly across the land.

In the seaport of Kiel, the old and renowned university was a scene of Nazi destruction. From the library, cartloads of precious books were hauled out to be burned. A man in uniform read the list of condemned authors as hundreds of volumes were tossed into the flames. Heinrich Heine, Albert Einstein, Sigmund Freud—at the reading of each name, wild cheers rang out.

Somewhere down the list came the name of Franz Boas, and his books were fed into the bonfire. At this same university, only a few years earlier, the anthropologist had been honored with a doctoral degree.

For the Nazi regime, Franz Boas was a distinct threat.

It was Boas's enlightening studies of human races which challenged the Hitler race theory. And the Nazis were building an elaborate system of doctrines on which they would soon justify their dictatorship, their aggression against other nations, the murder of some six million "non-Aryans," the plunging of the entire world into war.

Warning that "the whole world is aflame," the aged Dr. Boas called his fellow scientists into action. He pleaded that the truth about race could not lie buried in obscure scientific journals while the world needed popular education. Half-paralyzed, the little professor made his voice heard wherever he could.

He branded the Nazi theories as racism, which he defined as "the ready belief in the superiority of one race over another." Boas pointed out that racial bigotry in both the United States and in Germany had the same roots.

The Nazis seemed to copy their campaigns against the Jews from America's treatment of black people. Under Nazi law, the German Jews were strictly segregated from the rest of the population, forbidden to intermarry with non-Jews, barred from many kinds of jobs, schools, and living areas. They were deprived of voting and other civil rights, subjected to mob attacks. Further, they were branded as mentally inferior and morally unfit.

In America, black people had always been easily recognized victims because of their dark skins. But physical appearance alone was not enough to distinguish a Jew from an "Aryan." This difficulty was readily overcome by the Nazis in their terror campaign. Every Jew was required to wear a clearly visible badge, which marked him out for discrimination.

As in America, the racists in Germany seemed hardly troubled by the fact that their theories made little sense. The "race" they glorified was the Aryan—not a race at all but a group of ancient tribes from southeast Russia that invaded India in 1500 B.C. The Nazis concentrated their violence against the Jewish "race"—which is also not a race but a people who in ancient times shared a common living space, a religion, a culture. Because the Japanese and the Italians joined them in their war efforts, the Nazis were willing to proclaim them honorary members of the Aryan "super-race."

The Nazis repeated the false notions that were still being widely taught in the United States—that race determines mentality. In the official Hitler program was this dogma: "Race sets its imprint on man's spiritual features no less than on his outward form. It determines his thoughts and perceptions, his powers and instincts. It decides his character and his nature."

With this as a basic doctrine, the Nazis divided people into "superior" and "inferior" races. By official policy, "lower races" did not deserve to be treated as though they were human. Once "non-Aryans" were defined as a lower order of beings, there was no longer any stopping place. On a wave of race hatred, the German people followed the Nazi leadership blindly, madly. They took part in the slaughter of millions in death camps and gas chambers. Racism had run its full course.

Hitler proved that the doctrine of "super-race" can be directed against any people, anywhere. The Nazi armies became the torch-bearers of "racial purity." In the name of race supremacy, they marched against the Poles and the Czechs, the Dutch and the French, the English and the Russians, the Norwegians and the Americans.

As the nightmare of Nazism unfolded, mankind learned to its horror where racism leads. That doctrine serves the interest of one violent, aggressive group at the expense of all others. Hitler's race theories fed the German hopes of glory while countless men, women, and children died, and the world was set aflame. Clearly, racism is a breeder of war.

In an unguarded moment of frankness, Hitler confessed: "I know perfectly well that in the scientific sense, there is no such thing as race. As a politician, I need something which enables me to abolish the old order. And for this purpose, the conception of race serves me well."

The Nazi race theory was not the pure invention of Adolf Hitler. His ideas were a patchwork gathered up from many sources. From the American example he learned how effective racist theories can be if they are presented in the name of science.

However, the truth had to be destroyed first. Whatever new scientific discoveries had been made about the human species, the actual meaning of races, the hard-won knowledge about the true nature of man—all these the Nazis put to the torch.

And yet, even in those troubled times when Nazi propaganda was being spread worldwide, men were still pressing toward enlightenment and freedom from mind-enslaving falsehoods. The antiscience of Hitlerism was being challenged by patient research into man's origins. Scientists were busy digging into the dim past to find buried evidence about man's beginnings and the formation of races, the diversity as well as the oneness of the human species.

Out of the Past

Scientists of the 1930s worked at widening the window into the anthropological past.

Those who peered through it might see strange and sometimes frightening wonders. Extinct beasts appeared there in sizes and shapes only vaguely resembling modern species. And men, what of them?

The newest fossil discoveries of the decade showed that Africa was probably the earliest home of man. From meager bits of fossil evidence, scientists were busy piecing together the story of *Homo sapiens,* his developing culture and his restless movements.

As gatherers and hunters, Stone Age men moved constantly in search of food. Travel may have been slow, but over hundreds of thousands of years, men widened their explorations and migrations.

Before their wanderings became extensive, human beings did not vary widely. They were a relatively small group, close-knit and intermingled. It must have been much later in the human experience that race came into existence. By then man had already developed his humanness. His brain was fully evolved. Artful and inventive, he enjoyed a complex social life, a many-sided culture.

How did races originate? All their digging into the human remains furnished scientists with few clues to answer that bewildering problem. In their quest, they turned to the findings of biology and the search that had begun with Darwin's *Origin of Species.*

A species is a closed group of interbreeding organisms. Darwin and those who followed him showed that when a population is cut off geographically from the rest of the species, it tends to become genetically different. In the isolated group new hereditary traits may appear. If these traits provide a more successful life style in the new environment, the isolated group evolves into what Darwin called a favored race.

Where and when did mankind begin to undergo such a

process? The scientists could only guess at the possibilities. The visible traits of races seemed to offer no simple explanations. Was it possible that a skin color or a type of hair might give an isolated population some survival advantage in a particular environment, so as to become an adaptive trait? It seemed clear that a dark skin was useful in screening out the burning rays of the hot sun. But a changed skin color as a new genetic trait of a population could only come about as part of the long-time processes of evolution, of natural selection. A sun tan is not inherited. But genes for dark or light skin tones might be spread throughout an entire population if either proved to be an advantage in survival.

The origin of races has long remained a matter of much scientific speculation. One possible line of thinking might go like this: In some ancient age, a band of dark-skinned migrants may have wandered northward from the tropical home base of mankind. Perhaps these wanderers settled in northern Europe, remaining isolated from other men over many generations.

Through diseases and hardship, this population may have been reduced to a dwindling group. The illness? Possibly a disease resulting from a deficiency of Vitamin D.

There were perhaps some few among the survivors who chanced to be born with skin of a lighter color. These were favored individuals in the special conditions of their life in the north. Their light skin afforded them a maximum of ultraviolet light from the sun, a source of Vitamin D.

Naturally, these healthier individuals not only thrived but also had larger families, who inherited their lightness of skin. Gradually, such a population might tend to become increasingly light skinned in one flourishing generation after the next. Skin color alone does not make a race. But the genes common to this population might set it on the path toward becoming a people of distinct appearance.

Under such a set of circumstances, this growing population not only carried forward the skin-color traits, they also spread among their offspring the full set of heritable characteristics which were present among the tiny group of "founders" of the new race.

The period of forming new human races was probably over when widening movement and travel between populations ended their isolation. At that time began an era of racial mixing that has continued until the present day.

For thousands of years, peoples have moved unceasingly about the earth in great migratory waves. Men drifted in pursuit of game and in search of some Eden beyond the next hillcrest. They traveled as invaders and as fugitives. Often they fled from tyranny and bondage. They escaped from natural disasters and from living environments which they themselves had helped to degrade.

Mongoloids crossed a land bridge into the American continents. Through the corridor of the Nile valley, Negroid populations moved northward. Europeans, Asians, and Africans carried on centuries of shifting warfare over that section of the world now known as the Middle East. Australia and the islands of the Pacific were discovered and occupied by people whose origins are lost in prehistoric time.

As history began to be written, tribesmen from the European steppes were pressing southward, as well as to the west and east. Successive far-reaching empires of Egyptians and Mongols, Huns and Moors, Greeks and Romans swept across the Old World. Races long separated came together —as in the Age of Discovery when Europeans met with central and southern Africans, with Orientals, with the Indians of the New World.

As active migrants, men merged their cultures—and their genes as well. The meeting of different ethnic and racial groups readily brought about widespread intermarriage and the mixing of populations. If ever there were any "pure" races, they have long since vanished. The ancestry of every person alive today goes back through ages of mankind's wanderings across the face of the earth.

One race, or racial stock, seemed to persist on each of the Old World continents of Africa, Europe, and Asia. But no race can be set off as a distinct unit clearly defined by geography. Nor can any man be biologically classified as a "purebred" member of a particular race. The races of man shade gradually into one another. Between them are many mixed and intermediate types.

A long overland journey from the beaches of Ghana in Africa to Korea's Pacific shore would reveal how continuous and overlapping are the human types. On such a straight-line course, the traveler would meet many native African, Arab, Caucasian, Siberian, Chinese, Korean peoples. Along the journey there are no points where "blackness," "whiteness," "yellowness" begins or ends.

There are no natural borderlines for races. Such boundaries, where they do exist, are in the minds of men— sometimes drawn on maps, or laid down by law, or enforced by threats and violence. Such artificial boundaries have long existed in American cities.

Black Ghetto

In the Middle Ages, Jews were required to live within walled sections of European cities—prisoners of prejudice. Such a district was called a ghetto.

In the Chicago of 1939, the term was put to a new use. Two young Negro men were engaged in a sociological study of one section of the city strikingly similar to the medieval ghetto. Its inmates were the black residents of Chicago.

St. Clair Drake and Horace Cayton were themselves inhabitants in what they called the black ghetto. Their families had come as migrants to a city that promised a livelihood and a better way of life. But in the 1930s, there were no jobs. The Great Depression gripped the nation for almost a decade. Few families in all America escaped the blows of the long crisis. Black people felt the worst of the economic whiplash.

A series of emergency efforts by the federal government brought some relief. The most significant of these was the Works Project Administration, a makeshift program that kept millions of people from complete idleness and starvation. One out of every four adults in Chicago's black community was without employment in private industry, either jobless, or "on WPA." It was WPA that sponsored a scientific study of that community, directed by Drake and Cayton.

The two young men, college trained in the social sciences, began what was to become a detailed examination of a single black urban community. In their book *Black Metropolis,* they told a factual story, without straining to draw sympathy for the plight of the Negro. However, it emerged as a portrait of a Jim Crow "town within a town."

The ghetto was a long, narrow rectangle of eight square miles in the dead center of Chicago. Here, some 300,000 black people lived in a clearly defined enclosure.

Thousands had migrated to Chicago by way of railroads from the South. They hardly suspected that the very railroad tracks which brought them into the city would form the main boundaries within which they would be forced to live out their lives.

East of the ghetto, "the tracks" separated the black community from the lakefront properties owned by rich white people. On the west, a long railroad embankment divided the ghetto sharply from the neighborhoods of Irish and Polish workers. The ghetto was also blocked off north and south.

Actually, the walls of the ghetto were not made of steel and concrete but of something far more rigid. Negro residents were enclosed by "the color line." This was a divider based on the myth that "superior" people lived on one side and "inferior" people on the other. The line was defined and defended by white people, powerfully supported by local government, real estate and other business interests, banks, and the city's leading cultural institutions.

A black man who managed to hold a job in the slag yard of a steel mill or in the hog kill of the stockyards might leave the ghetto during his working hours. A black woman might labor as a maid in the homes of the wealthy. But nightfall found the masses of Negroes back within the walls of the restricted South Side community.

It was constant pressure by white people that kept the black ghetto intact. White rules, written and unwritten, forbade the Negroes from living beyond the edges of the enclosure. The ghetto was, in fact, made and maintained by whites. Certainly it was not the creation of blacks.

As Drake and Cayton described it in scientific terms, the ghetto was revealed as a home of extreme hardship. Here was overcrowding in dwellings that showed the evidence of having been lived in for too long by too many people. Poor health and shortened lives were the natural result of ghetto conditions. Schools and the whole range of city services were obviously inadequate, in sharp contrast to those in the rest of the city.

In the harsh years of the 1930s, the Negroes of Chicago's South Side tried to become a self-sustaining community. Efforts were made to bolster the struggling business firms owned by black people. "Spend your money where you can work," was a popular slogan.

When families were evicted for nonpayment of the high rents and their belongings dumped into the streets, "flying squads" of black men and women moved the ousted families back into their homes. The South Side community pooled its political strength and sent the only black congressman to Washington. The people tried to exert some control over their own lives.

Within the walls, the ghetto bore its own bitter fruit. What grew there was a sense of unity among black people, rising from their own shared suffering. From the soil of the Jim Crow community flourished a new spirit of black self-consciousness and militancy.

"The inhabitants of the Black Ghetto grow restless in their frustration, penned in, isolated, overcrowded," Drake and Cayton wrote. "While it is conceivable that many Negroes would prefer to live in an all-Negro community, they resent being forced to live there."

A kind of fierce pride was rising among the residents of the ghetto. Many turned inward toward their own people, shaping a way of life that was distinctly theirs. An urban black culture was developing, linked to the rural South, but with deep roots in African origins.

As for the city's whites, they knew little about life within the "Black Metropolis"—and cared less. During the daylight hours, the white man entered the ghetto as landlord and merchant, as policeman and social worker, as bill collector and political boss.

In those years, agreements were signed in the white

neighborhoods of the city which pledged owners not to sell or lease property there "to any member of a race not Caucasian." Chicago was soon to echo with gunfire and bomb blasts. A series of riots, sieges, and burnings erupted wherever black families tried to move into so-called white neighborhoods.

The racial boundary lines were being patrolled by terror. Guilt-haunted and hate-crazed, white men turned violent. They saw each attempt by a Negro to leave the ghetto as an invasion of their domain. In horror, they pictured him coming into the white community and bringing the black ghetto with him—the very ghetto that whites had invented.

The Chicago situation was not unique. The grim story of Drake and Cayton's *Black Metropolis* was being repeated in city after city. The urban Jim Crow scene in America was one of white neighborhoods and white suburbs, enclosing a central black core.

More and more, the entire nation was being split into two groups, which government census reports labeled white and nonwhite. And those same labels even showed up soon on life-giving supplies of human blood!

ERA OF STRIFE

"E Pluribus Unum"

Lights burned late in the Washington office of Dr. Charles Drew during the stormy first months of 1941.

Europe lay in the darkness of war. On World War II battlefields and in the bomb-battered British cities, the toll of casualties was high. A blood transfusion often made the difference between life and death. And supplying human blood to the war fronts was the special task of Dr. Drew.

He was a strikingly handsome black man in his early forties, with the build of a college athlete, a champion in five sports. However, it was in scientific research and in surgery that Dr. Drew distinguished himself. His main work became centered in blood transfusion, the method of transferring the life-sustaining fluid to persons in need of it.

Young Dr. Drew was a rare combination. Along with his scientific talents, he had a superb record as an administrator. Few black men in America were succeeding on ordinary merits alone. Extraordinary ability, with plenty to spare, had placed Dr. Drew in full charge of the American Red Cross blood program.

Blood transfusion was by then a well-established medical procedure. But it was not until World War II that nations were confronted with blood problems on a new and vast scale. Huge quantities of blood were required. Moreover, the problems of shipping, handling, and storing blood demanded new techniques. The use of whole blood could not meet these needs.

It was Dr. Drew who did the outstanding research in

140

using plasma as a substitute for whole blood. His original answers to the problems made possible a far-ranging system of blood banks. Under his direction, thousands of people were able to give blood which would then be processed, stored, shipped across the ocean and delivered to war casualties—all under antiseptic conditions.

On the war fronts, death was choosing victims with no regard for Hitler's doctrines of race. Throughout America, the call was out for blood donors without restrictions as to their racial origins. In February 1941 America was not yet in the war but would be before the year was out. It was in that month that the American Red Cross began building its storage of blood supplies to meet the country's wartime needs.

For Dr. Drew, these were hectic, work-filled days. He tried to get in a few quiet moments of thought before each frantic day began. And only his secretary was in the office when he arrived early one morning. An official-looking message from the War Department was already on the doctor's desk.

From out of the blue, the army had dropped its bomb. Its orders were final. Henceforth, all blood would be strictly segregated—according to race!

Because of the army's order, innocent men, women, and children would die. Out of sheer bigotry people could not give life blood to each other. Drew's own blood could not be offered to a fellow American!

That morning, newsmen crowded into Dr. Drew's office. He longed to cry out to them in rage. Instead, his words were calm and measured. Outwardly he was the medical specialist, performing a difficult task with full self-control.

"I am speaking to you today not as a Negro but as a scientist," he told the newsmen. "There is absolutely no scientific basis to indicate any difference in blood according to race." In answer to a question, he replied that the army's edict was "insulting, immoral, and unscientific."

Dr. Drew resigned from his position, left the blood program—and never looked back. A brilliant man was lost to the nation's service in a critical hour.

Racism worked its strange and terrible ways in the very midst of a war for democracy. Donors with the "wrong" skin color were turned away at blood banks across the nation. And others with a different "wrong" skin color were soon being rounded up and locked up.

War Fever

For a young American named Fred, life suddenly changed on a March day in 1942.

Fred didn't quite know what had hit him. A native of Oakland, California, he grew up in the bayside town and went to school there. Fred learned a trade and held a good job in the shipyards. He and his girl were planning to be married. Things changed when Fred learned he was wanted by the police.

The trouble was that Fred's last name was Korematsu. And from a close look at his face, it could be seen that his ancestry was Japanese. America was at that moment at war with three countries—Germany, Italy, and Japan. For reasons that were still not very clear, every person on the West Coast with Japanese forebears was being arrested.

For Fred Korematsu the swift flow of events was bewildering. It was not his country that had bombed Pearl Harbor. *His* country was the United States. He had never been in Japan in his life. He could neither read nor write Japanese.

With the country at war, the Boilermakers Union had canceled Fred's membership because of his race. The American-born young man had lost his job in the shipyard. These were the first of many strange things which were to happen.

It was all like some nightmare, and Fred lay awake trying to sort out the meaning of it all. He was filled with shame that the country of his birth would consider him an enemy! Whether he could marry his fiancée, a girl of European ancestry, was now in question. The prospect ahead was probably years of detention until the war's end—and then what?

The slight physical difference between himself and any white man—just how important was it? And couldn't it somehow be erased? Only that morning Fred Korematsu had planned to change his name and to have some plastic surgery done to alter his features—then somehow to lose himself in the white world. But it was too late. Every man, woman, and child with Japanese ancestry throughout the West was being rounded up. In the next days, Fred Korematsu found himself confined in an enclosure at Tanforan Racetrack.

Amid drab surroundings, a hundred thousand uprooted people were moved into makeshift quarters, many at fairgrounds and racetracks. Families lived in former stock pens and horse stalls. In time, the exiles were distributed to ten detention camps in remote western wasteland areas. People from all walks of life were thrown together in tar-papered barracks, and kept there by armed guards, high walls, barbed wire.

The outbreak of war had unloosed panic and prejudice on the West Coast. Taking the lead, the American Legion demanded that all "Japs" be imprisoned. The state's big agricultural organizations insisted that Japanese farmers and fruit growers be interned. West Coast newspapers joined in the outcry against the "Yellow Peril." All the old racial slurs against the Japanese people were revived.

In the war hysteria that followed, rapid-fire rumors spread widely. A humble Japanese gardener was charged with carrying a short-wave transmitter in his garden hose. A naval sentry was sure he had seen light signals from the house where a Japanese family lived. Two Oriental men were arrested with road maps in their possession. White farmers published fears that the Japanese fruit and vegetable growers were planning to poison the nation's food supply. Dozens of fanciful accounts were spread about so-called signaling devices set up by the Japanese. A white mob plowed up a field of blossoms, claiming that the Japanese grower "had planted his flowers in a way that when viewed from a plane, they formed an arrow pointing to the airport."

These and thousands of similar charges all proved to be unfounded. After careful checking by the FBI, not a single act of spying or sabotage by Japanese-Americans could be proved. But this in itself was very suspicious! As the top army commander in the area, General John DeWitt warned: "The very fact that no sabotage has taken place is a disturbing and confirming indication that such action *will* be taken."

There were some white Americans who questioned the special mistreatment of the Japanese. While the United States was also at war with two other countries, there was no such wholesale round-up of people of German or Italian descent. By contrast, sweeping orders against the Japanese included native born and foreign born, citizens and non-citizens alike.

The disturbing questions were answered in racist language by General DeWitt, "The Japanese race is an enemy race and while many second and third generation Japanese, born on American soil, possessed of United States citizenship have become 'Americanized,' the racial strains are undiluted."

Government officials brushed aside questions as to why the United States for the first time in its history was arresting whole families on no criminal evidence, without charges or trials. They denied hotly that people were being put into "concentration camps." Only the Nazis did things like that!

Strange and terrible events occur in wartime. In the hate-filled passions of the moment, ordinarily sane men perform violent deeds. Responsible leaders do things they will later regret. What part does underlying racism play in some of these actions? Would these same acts have been committed against members of the white race? America has never wanted to face up to those kinds of questions—if indeed there are any answers.

It was Fred Korematsu who drew some strong responses from the United States Supreme Court in one of the test cases that finally ended the Japanese internment after more than two years. Justice Frank Murphy declared that the approval by the lower courts of the seizure of Japanese civilians was "a legalization of racism."

Justice Robert H. Jackson added, "Korematsu has been convicted of an act not commonly a crime. It consists merely of being present in the state whereof he is a citizen, near the place where he was born, and where all his life he has lived." He charged that Korematsu and the thousands who suffered with him were victims of "racial discrimination."

By August 6, 1945, both Germany and Italy were defeated. Tottering and doomed, Japan tried to carry on the war alone against the combined Allied forces.

At 9:15 A.M. that morning, a lone American bomber, high over the Japanese city of Hiroshima, dropped a single bomb and roared away. Forty-three seconds later, the parachuted bomb exploded in the center of the city. In a single, unearthly flash, Hiroshima was leveled. Men, women, and children within miles were killed. Three days later, a similar atomic bomb destroyed Nagasaki. In the two raids, more than 100,000 people perished instantly. Thousands were to die later from burns and radiation.

More than a quarter of a century later, the harrowing questions of Hiroshima and Nagasaki still haunt the world. Couldn't the power of the A-bomb have been demonstrated in some other way? Did the United States have no alternatives for ending the war? Was the use of an atomic bomb necessary against cities in which all but a few victims were civilians? Did racism play any part in the A-bomb decision?

Statesmen and religious leaders, writers and educators joined in condemning the use of the A-bomb. Troubled by a deep sense of their own responsibility for making nuclear weapons available, many American scientists denounced the bombing of the Japanese cities.

In the postwar period came a new commitment of scientists to the urgent problems of society. Scientist and citizen could no longer afford to live in separated worlds. Surely the scientist had something very important to say about war and about its twin evil, racial bigotry.

A Scientist Serves

For Ruth Benedict, her long career at the side of Franz Boas had opened new scientific worlds. She remembered how at Columbia in the 1920s the great anthropologist had introduced her to the fascinating study of mankind's varied cultures. By the 1930s Boas had become completely caught up in activity responding to the threat of the Nazi use of racism as a weapon of destruction.

"Such a waste!" Ruth Benedict said of her beloved teacher and co-worker. "He has given up science for good works."

But now the 1940s had come, bringing world war and the slaughter of millions in Hitler's death camps. Ruth Benedict was suddenly aware that a scientist cannot be detached from the crucial problems of the times.

America was in turmoil, amid a world divided into two warring camps. This nation was lining up strongly against the fascist aggressors. But a few shrill voices could still be heard urging the United States to join with the Nazis and the forces of racial bigotry. Hitler's Germany, they said, was the fatherland of Nordic white supremacy, the foe of "inferior" races.

One of this country's most famous heroes, Charles A. Lindbergh, warned America against any action "which will reduce the strength of the White race." The transatlantic flier wrote in an article in the *Reader's Digest*, "It is time to turn from our quarrels and to build our White ramparts again. Our civilization depends . . . on a Western Wall of race and arms which can hold back either a Genghis Khan or the infiltration of inferior blood."

To such racist appeals, Ruth Benedict responded with

anger and fighting spirit. She had now achieved fame in her own right. And as a noted anthropologist, Dr. Benedict took on the task of educating the public on the meaning of racial bigotry and its link with war.

Hitler had made the connection very clear. Horrified by the Nazi example, Americans seemed ready for a deeper understanding of racism. The popular writings of Dr. Benedict filled a need.

Her scientific background in anthropological research fitted her well to deal with the pressing questions of race. From her studies of many human societies, she could draw the lesson that it is not race but culture "that really binds men together."

With precise scientific evidence, she demolished the Nazi claim that "race superiority is the secret of great civilizations." Each era of human history has seen outstanding achievements in every part of the world. And civilizations cannot be ranked on a simple scale of "better" or "worse."

In her writings, Dr. Benedict showed that western society is an example of how all races and past cultures contributed to the building of a new civilization. The invention of cities and written languages, sea and land transport, printing and metal-working, medicine and mathematics, the calendar and the compass—all these came out of varied societies with a wide range of racial backgrounds.

She described what happened to the cultures of other peoples that were considered "useless" by white Americans. The native Indian was deprived of his land and the mainstays of his life. "His culture collapsed about him like a house of cards," wrote Dr. Benedict, describing the ordeal of the American Indians.

Even more drastic was the change for the Africans who were enslaved, "most of them transported from Nigerian kingdoms with prized cultural achievements." Abducted and shipped to this country as prisoners, black people were stripped of their names, their languages, and the rich social heritage of their homelands, Dr. Benedict related. For obvious reasons, slave traders and slaveholders were anxious to hide the cultural accomplishments of black people from the eyes of white America.

Willowy and white-haired, Ruth Benedict was an outstanding scientist and teacher. But it was as a writer that she reached America's millions. Sensitive and imaginative, she was a poet gifted in the use of language.

For her it was not enough that the old myths of race had been disproved in the learned journals, in college classrooms, and in the scientific laboratories. These dangerous falsehoods continued to live among the millions of ordinary people, embedded deeply in their minds and their daily behavior. Ruth Benedict worked at making the scientific findings on race the property of everyone—not an easy undertaking.

In the newspapers of Monday, March 6, 1944, Americans read of the Allied successes on global battlefields. A strange item that morning also told how a congressional committee had made a "capture" of its own. The committee had seized 55,000 copies of an educational pamphlet written by Dr. Ruth Benedict and an associate in anthropology, Dr. Gene Weltfish.

The pamphlet, entitled *The Races of Mankind,* had been purchased by the government for distribution to American troops. It was a brief, clear explanation of races, written with the utmost scientific care. But a few racist congressmen objected vigorously to the pamphlet as a whole. In particular, they did not like the report of a survey which showed that there are Negroes who are the intellectual equals of whites.

Unwittingly, the congressmen were opposing the army's

use of data which had been gathered by the United States Army! In the pamphlet, authors Benedict and Weltfish had simply reported the results of the army intelligence tests of World War I days. In the testing, Negroes living in three northern states had done better than whites in three southern states.

The anthropologists made it clear that these differences in test scores had nothing to do with race. They explained:

> The white race did badly where economic conditions were bad and schooling was not provided, and Negroes living under better conditions surpassed them. The differences did not arise because people were from the North or South, or because they were white or black, but because of differences in income, education, cultural advantages, and other opportunities.

The congressmen stood firm over their captured pamphlets. They vowed that such information must be withheld from the men in the armed forces—who were just then fighting a war against the Nazi upholders of racial bigotry!

The war had somehow brought to a crisis the tormenting ailment of our society. Rejecting Nazi racism, we still seemed eager to retain the special American variety. The democracy that we preached to the world did not quite fit the pattern of what we practiced at home.

Horned Beast

A dilemma is a two-horned creature. And in the 1940s, such a dangerous beast was at large in this land.

Responding to a call for help in dealing with the monster, Gunnar Myrdal arrived in the United States. He was a Swede with an outstanding record as a social scientist.

Dr. Myrdal made a six-year study of America, sponsored by a private corporation with the aid of government and state officials, as well as many specialists in all phases of life in the United States. His opinions on what was afflicting this country were released in two large volumes entitled *An American Dilemma.*

The book was more fact than opinion. It was a thorough and thoughtful report on every aspect of the Negro-white experience in America. Myrdal did not spare his readers or shield them from shocks. The nation was in serious trouble.

White Americans liked to think they lived by a high-minded code of conduct. They clutched to their bosoms the Golden Rule and the Ten Commandments, the Four Freedoms and the ten-point Bill of Rights. Liberty and equality were the ideals to which the country pledged its allegiance—and Myrdal called all this the American Creed.

However, the treatment of black people violated the country's most sacred documents and doctrines. As the Swedish scholar saw it, the nation was caught on the horns of this dilemma.

"The status accorded to the Negro in America," he wrote, "represents a century-long lag in public morals." Myrdal was convinced that Americans could not continue their double life. He saw this nation flaunting the banner of democratic freedom while at the same time trampling it underfoot. America was torn, the Swedish scholar said, by this "ever-raging conflict."

Myrdal's book was a mirror. And somehow a good many Americans summoned up the strength to look into it and see themselves honestly. Myrdal was purposely brought in from a distant land as a skillful but unbiased observer of some ugly truths about this nation. Undoubtedly it was an act of courage for Americans to summon a specialist to examine the inner reality of Negro-white relations. At least they were ready to have the social scientist study the conditions—even if they were not yet ready to follow his advice.

"The ordinary man's ideas have not kept up to those of the scientist," Myrdal pointed out. But he did seem to see signs that in America "the popular race dogma is being victoriously pursued into every corner and effectively exposed." He was encouraged to find that wherever he went in this land the young people held "somewhat fewer superstitious beliefs" about race.

Myrdal helped to jar a number of citizens, who organized for action. And toward the end of the 1940s the federal government began to adopt some long overdue legislation on civil rights.

An American Dilemma showed clearly that racism was a man-made institution—and men could get rid of it. But time would prove the Swedish scholar overly confident in his view of how rapidly white people would settle their painful ordeal.

In finishing his study Myrdal realized that perhaps he had concentrated his attention on the wrong people. What had long been considered the "Negro problem" was in fact "a white man's problem," he pointed out. To find solutions, it was necessary "to give primary attention to what goes on in the minds of white Americans."

In every possible manner, declared Myrdal, the white American tried to twist out of responsibility for the human suffering in the segregated black world. But nothing could make it disappear from his mind. Even in his "restricted" community, his racially "pure" suburb, the white resident could not blot out the vision of black Americans, oppressed and degraded. Wherever he fled, the white man was confronted with his own guilt.

He might "explain" until doomsday, but he had to face someday the contradictory double world of his own making, free and unfree, privileged and underprivileged. He had created conditions for other people which he would not tolerate for himself.

The facts were too obvious to deny. Myrdal revealed an America of segregated neighborhoods and schools, "white only" restaurants and theaters, Jim Crow trains and buses. Discrimination was keeping black people in poverty. Even if he had skills comparable to those of the white worker, the Negro was losing out. Government figures clearly showed the average black man was being cheated of half his lifetime earnings. Racism reduced his life span by an average of ten years.

At the same time, Americans sang a hymn to the "sweet land of liberty" and an anthem that called it "the land of the free." This was a nation "conceived in liberty and dedicated to the proposition that all men are created equal." Americans pledged allegiance to a flag representing "liberty and justice for all." *E Pluribus Unum*, read the Latin words on the American coin. The motto means "From Many—One." The idea ran deep in our democratic heritage. But racism was the other side of the coin.

Another favorite image was America as the melting pot where all differences mixed and merged. The pot simmered—but something else was cooking.

INTO THE FIFTIES
"Mankind Is One"

The 1950s were the years when America's melting pot boiled over. In the cities, the newer generations of immigrant families were pouring out of their old neighborhoods.

With growing prosperity Italians and Poles, Irish and Greeks resettled in better communities and spread out into the suburbs. Once hated and barred, they would now have little trouble finding their way into the mainstreams of American life.

But the flow was sharply cut off for those with darker skins. The new opportunities stopped abruptly at the color line.

Black ghettos were growing in population but not in living space. A great migration was under way, and by the end of the decade, there would be more Negroes living in the North than in the South. But in the northern cities, the intense pressure of racism kept the black population confined. Even if they had the money for good housing, black families were not permitted to leave the ghettos. Those who sought homes in new communities were turned back by seething race hatred.

Strangely, the most violent of the whites were often those who had recently suffered discrimination themselves. In Chicago and Detroit, Baltimore and Houston, the fire-bombs sounded in the nights. Often the screeching epithets hurled at Negro families were pronounced with a foreign accent.

On World War II battlefields, the white soldiers usually got along well with the blacks with whom they fought side-by-side. They had a common enemy. Oddly, in peacetime America these same white veterans often attacked the blacks fiercely. The common enemy was gone. Instead, the white ex-soldiers saw the blacks as "the enemy" in their own struggle for jobs, financial security, safe home investments, control of schools and communities.

Along with the blacks, others who could be stamped with the stigma of "inferior race" suffered as well. Mexican-Americans and Puerto Ricans ran into the hard barriers of racist bigotry. In the large cities, people with Spanish surnames found themselves barred from many types of employment, segregated into poor districts, treated as social outcasts.

As the second half of the twentieth century opened, new studies were being made of the hatreds and fears which beset this nation. Psychology offered some hope of understanding the workings of hostile groups. The social psychologist pondered the why of America's racial problems. Could any sense be made out of anything as senseless as race hatred? Were there any orderly scientific principles that could be applied to the disorder of mobs rioting?

A systematic search for the sources of racial bigotry turned first to the nursery. Thousands of infants were tested and proved to be free of any inborn racial prejudice. The studies of growing children showed something else.

Before they were out of diapers, white children were being taught the first lessons in discrimination. By the time they reached school, youngsters in America could tell at a quick glance who were the "good" people and who were the "bad." They had learned to prejudge, to use prejudice.

A particular culture may encourage strong loyalties to "my family," "my team," "my neighborhood," "my town," "my national group," "my race." America fostered such strong competitive attitudes and pride in one's own group. People growing up in this culture seemed to draw much satisfaction from their group being the "best." Thinking racially, the white American grew up with a picture in his mind of the various races of mankind vying through the ages, striving to "get ahead." And who was it that had proved to be the winner of the contest, the superman? Why, it was he himself—the white man!

This fantasy had many uses. It seemed to give white men the right to exploit others, to use and treat them in almost any way supremacists saw fit. In America they certainly had the power to do so. Being the majority, whites had little trouble enforcing their rules.

To support the myth of white superiority, a number of additional myths had been invented. The most important of these was the notion that members of all other races were born inferior. This dogma was supported, in turn, by false images of each "nonwhite" race, and applied to every individual member.

These mythical models or stereotypes included fixed patterns of behavior—even though scientists had shown clearly that behavior is learned and not inborn. However, treating dark-skinned people as though they were inferior had one important effect. For a biased white society to deny that Negroes could make it in America was a prophecy that seemed to fulfill itself. The more whites viewed Negroes as inferior, the more they insured for the black population a position far down on the scale of American life. To this kind of process, social psychologists give the name "vicious circle." Thus, while race did not really determine the way people behaved, racism actually did!

Studies disclosed that race prejudice was widespread throughout all of white America. But individual attitudes varied. The psychologists also showed that one kind of white attitude criticized the Negro for behavior which actually stemmed from Jim Crow conditions. However, others held to a racist belief in the biological inferiority of black people.

A great many white people were unaware of their own prejudices or never faced them squarely. Some whites kept their bias to themselves. Others openly voiced racist ideas, but performed no open racist acts. And still others were not only rabid in their views but also ready to take part in discriminatory activity of many types.

Such probing research into prejudice and discrimination helped to shape the program of action known as the civil rights movement. Its activity was aimed at stopping overt acts of discrimination. These efforts sought laws which would make it illegal to deny to Negroes their civil rights. This was a method of getting at some of the most immediate problems of black people—jobs, housing, education.

"We cannot convince the white man to overcome his prejudices," the civil rights movement seemed to say, "but we can stop his discriminatory acts."

While this program achieved important gains, it was in a sense an admission of failure to reach the minds of white Americans. The social psychologists offered no easy solutions. Their studies showed, in fact, that prejudices were stubborn and did not yield readily to logic or reason.

The second half of the century had begun. And with it came a massive and worldwide scientific assault on the dogmas of racism. Biologists and psychologists, anthropologists and sociologists were at work on the problems—as never before.

Meeting of Minds

"Scientists have reached general agreement that mankind is one."

This proclamation was heard round the world. In Paris, a large gathering of learned men and women had worked long and hard over a joint statement. At last, the vote that went around the long green-covered table was yes, spoken in a variety of languages.

On July 18, 1950, the United Nations Educational, Scientific and Cultural Organization, UNESCO, published its "Statement on Race." After centuries of confusion and conflict, here for the first time was a concise summary of mankind's common knowledge about races. The statement also marked a realization that racism was still a serious global problem.

In Germany that year, the trials were being completed of those Nazi leaders who had committed terrible racist crimes. After centuries of white colonialism, Africa and Asia were crackling with racial tension. In 1950, the dark-skinned people in French, British, Dutch, Belgian, and Portuguese colonies were in open revolt.

Apartheid, the policy of the Union of South Africa, was a system of segregation whereby a small white group exploited the huge black and "colored" population. In Latin America, whites, Indians, and Negroes had lived peacefully in mixed societies, but in 1950 sharp racial clashes broke out.

In the United States, "State's Rights" had become the slogan of white resistance to civil rights. Flaunting Dixie banners and shouting rebel yells, the upholders of white supremacy were on the march.

In response to persistent and worldwide racism, scientists had come to Paris to compare their findings about race. The series of statements that emerged from the UNESCO meetings varied somewhat in their scientific emphasis. But on the main points there was general agreement.

There were no "pure" races, the scientists agreed. The biological basis for classifying races was not mental qualities but only certain physical traits. One characteristic was common to all mankind regardless of race—the ability to learn and change. Differences among men or groups were no justification for denying human rights to any of them.

The 1950 statement declared:

From the biological standpoint, the species *Homo sapiens* is made up of a number of populations, each of which differs from the others in the frequency of one or more genes. Such genes, responsible for the hereditary differences between men, are always few when compared to the whole genetic constitution of man. . . . This means that the likenesses among men are far greater than their differences.

Those who met in Paris did not delude themselves. Science produced no magic wand that could wave away the deep racist hatreds and fears that festered in the minds of men. And yet the scientists felt somehow that their findings had some vital meaning for mankind.

Racism no longer has the support of science, they seemed to be saying. Those distinguished scholars from the United States who joined in the Paris discussion knew at first hand the turmoil of racial unrest. The Paris newspapers reported each day on the anti-Negro rioting at a housing site in South Chicago, at a public swimming pool in St. Louis, at a polling place in Dallas.

The issues would not be finally won in scientific conferences. Many would be fought out in the legislative halls and in the courts, in politics and on picket lines, in boycotts and marches, in the streets. But scientific knowledge added power and meaning to the effort to win civil rights. As more people came to understand that there were no inferior races, that knowledge spurred the campaigns against inferior schools, inferior housing, and inferior earnings for those with darker skins. The crusade for equality and for scientific truth marched arm in arm.

In a thousand arenas of man's age-old struggle to move forward, science and reason have won out over ignorance and falsehood. Why couldn't the fight against racist bigotry be won as well? Why not bury the myth of "super-race" along with the countless other superstitions that science has destroyed? These questions echoed around the globe.

Meanwhile, at the United Nations headquarters in New York City, attention centered on another problem. The General Assembly in 1951 put into effect an agreement condemning the crime of genocide, the killing of national, racial, or religious groups.

The declaration was an outraged response by the nations of the world to the genocidal practices of the Nazis. The treaty made genocide an international crime, whether committed during peace or war. It was now up to each member nation to approve the genocide treaty—and to abide by its code.

During the next twenty years, the major nations of the world, seventy-five of them, would sign—with the exception of the United States. The United States Senate was unwilling to consent to the genocide treaty, even though this country had joined in drafting its rules.

The senators, prominently those from the South, stubbornly refused to sign the United Nations declaration for a variety of reasons. Some voiced open fears that under its provisions the United States would be the first to stand accused. They were especially wary of a clause condemning acts which cause "mental harm" to members of a racial group.

A Study with Dolls

To the casual visitor, the work of Clark and Clark might have seemed like child's play. But to this research team, the nursery school was a laboratory for a vital study of American life. The behavior in the preschool classes observed by the Clarks would later draw the close attention of nine elderly gentlemen, the justices of the Supreme Court of the United States.

A husband-and-wife team, Doctors Kenneth B. and Mamie K. Clark were studying how children see themselves. In particular they wanted to know how tiny tots look at skin color, their own and that of other children—and how they react to "race."

The experience with dolls was the most revealing activity of all. The dolls were identical—except that some were dark-skinned and others light-skinned. Day after day, the two psychologists carefully observed the children at play, occasionally offering a comment or asking a question.

"Give me the doll you like best," they would say, or, "Give me the doll that is the nice color." Carefully, the Clarks compiled the observed reactions of hundreds of children. The data added up to some startling conclusions.

At a very early age, black children already had received the disturbing message of American society: that to be black is "bad," and to be white is "good."

Dozens of other social psychological studies being carried on in the 1950s showed similar attitudes among white children. From the age of three onward, both black and white children in America were keenly aware of "race." They also knew they were living in a society which strongly favored white people.

Long before they learned to read, black and white children had observed certain facts about American life: that whites and blacks were kept separated in their neighborhoods, in churches, in schools; whites worked at a wide range of occupations and were generally the professional people, managers, and owners; blacks were to be found in the serving and laboring jobs, usually poor and unskilled and uneducated. Wherever he looked, the child could see that the white person held advantages and prestige, authority and power.

Generally, white children learned race prejudice not by associating with black people, but by contact with society's *ideas* about black people. In a thousand small ways, the social environment put its stamp of approval on whiteness.

Who teaches a child to hate and fear a member of another race? Psychological studies disclosed that such teachings came from a wide range of the child's own experiences—in the home, school, and church, and from television and movies.

Some white children in the South told a psychologist that they were sometimes punished by their parents when they and their playmates got into mischief. But the punishment was always more severe, they revealed, when they had been playing with black children.

Through subtle uses of language, white parents relayed their own prejudices to their small children, it was disclosed by a study of a white neighborhood adjoining a black community. The whites were always "we" and the blacks were "they."

In one revealing incident, Dr. Kenneth Clark recounted the words of a Negro six-year-old, carefully putting away the dolls at the end of the day, separating them by color. "The white and black should not be in one box," said the child soberly. "They fight, and the white doll always wins."

From their evidence, the social scientists were piecing together an ugly portrait of the racial attitudes and behavior of Americans, beginning at infancy. All persons need a sense of their own worth as human beings. But from their earliest years, black children were being denied the respect of American society. From the outset, their color put them at a disadvantage. Stripped of any recognition of their cultural heritage and their humanness, they soon became the victims of daily shocks, restrictions, insults, discrimination. To Dr. Clark it was clear that "the Negro child by the age of five is aware that to be colored in contemporary American society is a mark of inferior status."

The noted Negro psychologist pointed to studies which showed clearly that white children were damaged by racism as well. Among many white children, social scientists found a burden of anxiety and guilt, hatred and fear. Their prejudiced attitudes clearly left them less capable of dealing with a surrounding world which included a diverse range of people, most of them dark-skinned.

On the other hand, white children free from strong racist influences showed a greater ability to shape their own values of justice and fair play. They could respond to social problems in a more cooperative and reasonable way.

The nation's schools only reinforced the racist pattern. The most important task of the school system, many educators pointed out, was to teach children how to live in the spirit of democracy. But the most convincing everyday lesson of school life was often something else. Segregated along the color line, most schools taught that America did not really believe in the democracy it claimed to uphold.

In 1954, the Supreme Court of the United States made its unanimous decision in the case of *Brown* v. *Board of Education*. The historic ruling declared racial segregation in the schools illegal.

It was no ordinary Monday morning—May 17, 1954. The word from Washington spread across the land like a refreshing spring storm. A workday nation paused to hear the thunderous news, scarcely realizing the full meaning of the moment.

Almost a hundred years had passed since the Supreme Court had declared in the *Dred Scott* case that Negroes were "so far inferior that they had no rights which the white man was bound to respect." In the 1850s, white supremacy was not only a fact of everyday American life but the official policy of every branch of the government as well. In the *Brown* case of 1954, the doctrine of the master race was outlawed—even though the law of the land would be evaded and defied for years to come.

The nation could look back to a time when the inferiority of black people stood as an unchallenged American doctrine. But in the *Brown* case, the high court struck down "the policy of separating the races [which] is usually interpreted as denoting the inferiority of the Negro group."

Applied pointedly to the schools, the landmark decision had much wider significance. It implied that race could not be made the basis for treating any group as inferior beings.

Speaking of black children, the highest court of the land declared, "To separate them from others of similar age and qualifications solely because of their race generates a feeling of inferiority as to their status in the community that may affect their hearts and minds in a way unlikely ever to be undone."

The decision added, "This finding is amply supported by the evidence." And here, the justices pointed to a number of scientific studies on race. Some of the findings were listed in the Court's Footnote 11, which they attached to their decision. Included was the study of children made by Dr. Kenneth Clark.

Scientific research had made it possible to present the court with a clear warning about the effect of America's tragic racial blundering. Facing the overwhelming evidence, the justices made a complete change in the Supreme Court's policy.

Americans generally accepted the Court's decision. However, the response from many areas, both North and South, revealed how deeply the American people were infected by the old notions of race. Most of the southern states announced they would openly defy the law.

From Mississippi's Senator James O. Eastland came a howl of rage. "Never before has a Supreme Court relied on scientific authority," he cried out in the Senate.

In one branch of the government, the judiciary, the truth about race had been recognized at last. In another, the Congress, there was still much to learn.

A Star Is Born

For certain of its members the United States Senate was the last stronghold of white supremacy.

Yes, the racial exclusiveness of the Senate had been breached in the past, they admitted. In the years following the Civil War, two black senators had been elected from Mississippi. In 1928, the Senate was presided over by

Charles Curtis, Vice-President of the United States, and a former senator. Curtis's mother was the granddaughter of a Kansas Indian.

The Senate of the 1950s, however, was all white—and many of its members vowed that the upper house of Congress would remain that way. No wonder some strange things happened to them when the talk turned to Hawaiian statehood. Faces turned livid, neck veins bulged, and voices rose to a pitch of fury. Pages of the *Congressional Record* were filled with racist outpourings. One senator even fancied in horror that if admitted to the Union, Hawaii's representatives would be "heathen" Chinese, complete with pigtails and opium pipes!

Being of one species, all races of mankind can interbreed. And in Hawaii, they have. In few parts of the world were there to be found such a thorough mixture of racial strains. Polynesians, Caucasians, Chinese, Negroes, Filipinos, Japanese made up a mixed population. Intermarriage was the general pattern.

Hawaii had been a United States possession for more than fifty years. Rich in resources and situated on the main Pacific trade routes, the territory was highly valuable to the United States. But Congress balked at statehood.

"East is East and West is West," quoted the opposing senators, determined that the two should never meet as equals under the Stars and Stripes. The first statehood bill was introduced in 1919. It was only after forty years that the last debate in the long and hard-fought struggle for Hawaiian statehood began in January of 1959.

To the end, senators reviewed all the old racist arguments against the island inhabitants. But repeated scientific studies had been made among the residents which only reaffirmed the fact that the mixing of racial strains had produced a people of sound physical and mental health.

Research revealed that bad effects from intermarriage were due only to whatever racial prejudices existed in the social environment. But in Hawaii, mixed marriages were so common that they were an accepted part of life.

On a sparkling morning, August 21, 1959, bells chimed all over the sun-filled islands. A home-made American flag fluttered in the breeze, flaunting more stars than had ever been seen before. The fiftieth star was for Hawaii, the newly admitted state.

Within a few years, Hawaii would be represented in the United States Senate by two men of mixed ancestry, one with a Chinese name, the other Japanese. Even in the Senate, often called the world's most exclusive club, things were changing. But elsewhere in the United States, significant change was yet to come.

THE NINETEEN SIXTIES
"White Racism Is Responsible"

In one of the last hot spells of the year 1961, the State of Mississippi broke out its banners and bunting to celebrate Race and Reason Day.

The state capital at Jackson resounded with long-winded speeches. Special events took place among the fluttering Dixie flags that flew in Natchez and Hattiesburg, Greenwood and Vicksburg. The hero of the day was Carleton Putnam, a retired and aging businessman.

Putnam had written a book. In *Race and Reason*, he set out to prove once again that white men were born to be masters of the earth. The outworn dogmas were retold, dressed up in the scientific language of the 1960s. In place of the old rousing appeals to blind bigotry and dark passion, Putnam's stress was on "common sense."

In the 1960s, the KKK was still very active. Racist terrorism reached new levels, with the outright killing of civil rights leaders, the violent assaults on peaceful demonstrations, the bombing of Negro churches. But at the same time, racism was taking on a new guise. Putnam reflected a mood in the South which added a more "reasonable" approach to earlier types of rabid extremism.

The main thrust of the anti-Negro movement was now carried by the White Citizens Councils. These organizations appeared in every southern state, and established centers in many northern cities. They defended Jim Crow in the courts, tried to block the efforts of Negroes to register for voting, organized boycott campaigns to starve out whole black communities fighting for their rights. Powerful and well-financed, the White Citizens Councils directed the main attack on the Supreme Court decision that had outlawed segregation in the schools. They also sought to renew the discredited theories of white supremacy.

Fundamentally, racial bigotry is based on the notion of inferior and superior peoples. Scientists had examined that theory and discarded it. But men who had built careers and fortunes on race hatred would not let the matter rest there.

White Citizens Councils scoured the educational institutions of the South for learned men and women willing to lend their names to a new "scholarly" racism. At one Alabama college, they recruited a professor who wrote an anti-Negro article for a national magazine entitled "A Scientist's Report on Race Differences." A woman on another campus compiled a thick book which was supposedly a study of Negro intelligence. A former medical-school teacher in North Carolina was hired to write a paper showing that the anatomy of Negroes was inferior to that of whites.

A prize find for the racists was the retired Professor Henry E. Garrett, who had formerly been head of the department of psychology at Columbia University. Both Putnam and Garrett centered a fiery attack on the late Franz Boas as the man who had undermined America's long-standing doctrine of white superiority. Garrett blamed Boas for "the mixing of races," which he said, might eventually lead to the destruction of the world.

The White Citizens Councils employed several educators to write *A Manual for Southerners*, to be used in the public schools. "Scientists have studied the habits of different races," read the manual. "They find men's habits can be grouped by races." In reality, scientists had come to just the opposite conclusion—that a person's "habits" are not linked to his race but result from his acquired learning.

The main body of this country's scientists steadfastly rejected the new-style presentation of "the Southern point of view" on race. Leading societies and journals of American anthropologists and social psychologists, biologists, and sociologists joined in refuting the new claims.

They listed the basic errors of the racist group: mistakenly, a race was viewed as a permanent, fixed unit with a clearly defined, homogeneous membership; contrary to scientific findings, races were ranked as to quality; and inborn, genetic traits were confused with cultural characteristics, which stem from the social and environmental surroundings in which people live. Modern science offered no shred of evidence that might justify delaying the full freedom of black people for even a fleeting moment.

American science had come a long way since the days when ignorance and bigotry dominated its prevailing views on race. The slowly emerging truth had compelled learned men to revise their long-held views. Scientists, educators, historians were correcting the errors of the past and probing deeply into the true meaning of race. New insights were now possible.

In an earlier age, men like Jefferson and Lincoln could not go beyond the knowledge of their time. And the American history written in the nineteenth century could only reflect the limited understanding of that age. History is written by men, and often they record not only events but their own prejudices as well.

However, far into the twentieth century, there were still some prominent American intellectuals who clung to outworn and disproved doctrines. At the very time when the record of the nation's earlier years was being corrected by some historians, others were still writing from the standpoint of white supremacy. In the modern era, when most scholars had freed themselves from the old ignorance about races, the truth was still being twisted into the mold of bigotry.

Heedlessly, the anti-Negro race theorists proceeded in the opposite direction from the main trends of scientific research. Although in wild flight from the truth, they nevertheless had the sponsorship of powerful white institutions. They continued to expound their views, supporting their opinions by quoting each other at length. Occasionally, they found others who were not racists, but whose ideas they could use for their own purposes. One of these was the distinguished anthropologist Carleton S. Coon, of the University of Pennsylvania.

Repeatedly, Dr. Coon had gone on record as opposing any belief in inferior and superior races. However, in the 1960s the anthropologist produced a theory which gave white supremacists a foothold on which to rebuild an old and favorite argument.

For centuries, racists taught that white people had biological origins that were distinct from those of any other race. To the bigot, this old theory offered a ready explanation for racial differences, especially for the claim that some races were "more advanced" than others. Segregation was justified by the notion that Negroes and whites had arrived at their modern existence by differing biological paths, the old "several Edens" theory.

This view had been shattered by Darwin's explanation of the origin of species. However, Coon inadvertently gave the old racist theory new life. The anthropologist believed that *Homo sapiens* evolved not once but on at least five distinct occasions at five different locations. In 1962, Coon wrote the following:

> Over half a million years ago, man was a single species, *Homo erectus*, perhaps already divided into five geographic races or subspecies. *Homo erectus* then evolved into *Homo*

Sapiens not once but five times, as each subspecies living in its own territory passed a critical threshold from a more brutal to a more sapient state.

Coon went on to speculate that among the five subspecies, "those that crossed the evolutionary threshold the earliest have evolved the most," adding that they thereby reached higher levels of civilization. Coon theorized that Negroes were the last of the subspecies to be transformed into *Homo sapiens*.

Coon's theory was vigorously opposed by his fellow scientists. Biologists declared that Coon was offering "an extreme opinion, with no evidence of any nature to support it." Countless factors enter into even the slightest change, they pointed out, making it a unique event. It was hardly possible that man could have evolved independently more than once, let alone five separate times.

"Evolution is not repeatable," declared a leading American biologist, "because slight differences either in the environment or in the genetic materials might have resulted in something different from man."

However, Coon clung firmly to his viewpoint. Nor did he ever repudiate the racists, who were only too eager to use his name and make his theory their own. American racism had not altogether outworn its blood-stained KKK robes— but it was looking for a new mantle of academic and scientific respectability. Coon's words were repeated often in the tons of printed material circulated by the White Citizens Councils and in the radio and television programs which they sponsored.

As the decade of the 1960s moved on, the bigots not only revived a long-buried theory but also turned again to an old racist weapon—the so-called intelligence test.

Misused IQs

"If the Negro has an inferior mind. . ." That "if" has intrigued white men since the days of Thomas Jefferson.

If such a thing could be proven. . . why, the possibilities were many. Supposedly, such proof could justify almost any lower status for the black population of America—as second-class citizens, as servants, even as slaves.

A century ago, the "if" was being pondered by men measuring the sizes of skulls. In the late 1960s, the minds of black people were being measured again. This time the method was much more up to date than pouring buckshot into an empty cranium. The new trappings were the intelligence test, the Intelligence Quotient (IQ), and the computer.

Since they were first invented at the beginning of this century, intelligence tests have been widely used in the schools. They became the basis for classifying pupils. They have been used to measure learning progress. Efforts have also been made with such tests to direct young people toward suitable careers.

Many experts pointed out that IQ tests had limited usefulness and were being relied on much too heavily by the schools. Others favored the tests, and found them useful. All agreed, however, that the mental qualities revealed in IQ testing were a result of countless influences in the life of a child. The scores mirrored both the traits that a person had inherited from his parents and the learning acquired from the moment of birth.

No one could deny that individuals differed in mental ability. It appeared that there were some similarities of mentality among members of a given family. But it seemed impossible to say whether the main factor was heredity or whether it was the common set of social and environmental factors which may have prevailed within such a family.

However, to determine the genetic intelligence of an individual would be to measure his mental capacities before any cultural influences were brought into his life. Could any test be designed to measure intelligence at birth? And could inborn factors be separated from the influences of home, school, community, society?

To isolate heredity from environment and measure it in the human mind appeared to be an impossible undertaking. It would seem to be a task like that of finding a particular drop of water in a running stream. Nevertheless, the effort was being made in the 1960s.

At the University of California, a mild-mannered professor wrote an article which was soon to stir a storm of controversy. Arthur R. Jensen had acquired the results of some IQ tests taken by a group of California school children. Feeding the test data into his computer, he attempted to single out one factor—the portion of intelligence which had been genetically handed down to these school children by their parents. Jensen next divided the pupils into two groups, Negro and white, and compared test scores. From all this, he drew a neat conclusion—that the genes of Negro children made them less intelligent than white children.

Years of experience with intelligence tests had shown that they were some kind of yardstick—but no one seemed to be quite sure what they measured. One observation made by a great many experts was that a test score merely measured a person's ability to perform in one particular test. On that simple fact, Jensen had built an elaborate house of cards, condemning a whole race to inborn inferiority! Little wonder that Jensen's classing and ranking of genes by race was quickly challenged.

"There is not a shred of proof that the IQ tests are valid measures of native intelligence," one leading American psychologist declared, "and much proof that they are not."

The inventor of the intelligence test, Alfred Binet, had warned that the inborn intelligence of two individuals might be compared—but only if their lifetime experiences were the same. In America, skin color makes all the difference in a person's life. And it is rare to find a Negro and white child whose backgrounds are the same—or even similar. Many social scientists believe that blacks and whites in America actually live in two separate cultures.

Decades of experiments have revealed that intelligence-test results depended largely on the quality of the education that children had received. The worst scores anywhere in the United States were consistently those of children, Negro and white, who lived in those southern states with the poorest schools.

Test results also reflected differing economic and social backgrounds. They were no guide to the inherent mental ability of children who might be suffering from poor nutrition, who might need eyeglasses, or who were deprived of schooling by sickness. Nor could the test scores be adjusted to take into account the endless effects of poverty on children.

The results were also distorted by hidden problems of language. In the Southwest or in the Puerto Rican community of New York City, for example, the test questions posed special problems for children who spoke English in school and Spanish at home. In a race-conscious society, children were even affected by whether the person conducting the test was white or black.

And what about the true identity of the children whom Jensen classified so readily by race? What did he know about their genetic history, their ancestry? Many millions of Americans are of mixed backgrounds that may not be revealed by their physical appearance. In the sample groups used for his IQ testing, there was no way for Jensen to determine the precise racial origins of every child. A child identified by appearance as a Negro might have ancestors of whom the majority were either Negroid or Caucasoid.

Jensen erroneously assumed that whites and blacks in America were two biologically distinct groups whose genes could be compared in quality. There is no scientific basis for such a notion.

Often a good IQ test score merely shows that a child has mastered the knack of succeeding at tests. Experiments in the laboratory have proven that even monkeys and rats can learn skills in solving a problem or running through a maze.

Unfortunately, researchers sometimes try to deal with human beings as though they were experimental animals. Investigators have blundered again and again in oversimplifying the complex patterns in the human heart and mind. An endless number of unpredictable factors affects the performance of a child as he approaches a test.

Does he see any sense in taking it? What is his mood? How does a black child feel about his chances of competing with others, with white children? What rewards can he hope for in a racist society?

Often a black child may feel so hopeless that he doesn't care how high or low his test score will be. Such an attitude, and not native intelligence, is sometimes the real factor deciding the test score.

The over-all results of testing in America have shown that the range of IQ is the same for black and white. In both racial groups can be found children whose test scores are in the mentally retarded range as well as those at the "genius" level.

If anything, the Jensen results revealed how wide was the gap between black and white children—in terms of their opportunities, experiences, choices. But Jensen's strange conclusions only served to support those who were trying to widen the gulf!

To black observers, it seemed no accident that this new effort to downgrade black mental abilities came at a critical moment in the struggle for Negro rights. In the long, bitter experience of black people in America, "tests" too often had been the method used to deprive them of citizenship, the right to vote, the opportunity for schooling, the preferable job. It mattered little that the test now bore the label IQ. This was a familiar white man's device, used to "prove" blacks inferior.

In the 1960s, the mood of black America was changing. The black people were well aware of who it was that had long kept them in bondage—and they didn't want to be told that they were enslaved by their own genes! Neither IQ nor skin color was the true measure of a man's humanity. And the black man had grown tired of waiting to be recognized as a man.

A Man's Dream

In the hours just before dawn, it was cool and calm in the city of Birmingham, Alabama. The Reverend Martin Luther King, Jr., sat in a jail cell, writing.

This was Easter 1963. And King faced a morning of challenge. A brutal test of courage was being carried out in the streets of the southern steel city. All of black America looked on in a mood of rising anger and defiance. White

Americans, a great many of them, watched as well—with a sinking sense of shame.

Birmingham had unleashed all its racist fury against people asking for the simplest human needs. On television a startled nation saw men, women, and children savagely beaten by police, set upon by fierce dogs, hammered down with strong jets of water from fire hoses.

Both in and out of the local jail, King was at the center of this struggle, a capable and inspiring leader. This black man was bringing something entirely new to a nation that had always fought out its differences in a flow of blood, in a spirit of hatred. A man of religion, King felt a deep love for all mankind. His battle was not against enemies but against the evil that moved them. "If there is violence, it will not come from us," he said. But there was nothing weak or half-hearted in his style of direct action.

For whites and blacks as well, imbued with the old ideas of Negro inferiority, King arose as a new symbol of quiet dignity and deep determination. Strongly built and full-faced, appearing older than his thirty-four years, the Baptist minister was a man of fixed purpose and high faith. King typified a new spirit among black Americans.

Under his leadership, a drama of change was being acted out in the streets of Birmingham. Beginning with 1963, relations between the races would never be the same again. The "white problem" in America had suddenly reached a crisis. For blacks, there was an abrupt end to meekness and defeatism and patient waiting for freedom.

During the Easter days in Birmingham jail, King was kept in solitary confinement. But somehow he managed to give day-to-day leadership to the struggle in the streets.

The local white clergymen had denounced his efforts as "unwise and untimely." In the half-darkness of his cell,

King wrote a reply to them on scraps of newspaper, on toilet paper. This was to become the famous "Letter from a Birmingham Jail," one of the great documents of the civil rights movement. It was to mark the rising of a whole people from the mire of delay and postponement, from the slough of defeating "gradualism."

"We know through painful experience that freedom is never given by the oppressor," King wrote. "It must be demanded by the oppressed.

"For years now, I have heard the word, 'Wait.' It rings in the ear of every Negro with a piercing familiarity. This 'Wait' has always meant 'Never.' "

The embattled black leader pointed out that his people were beset by the most rabid and violent foes of American freedom. He did not appreciate the added harassment from those who called themselves friends, but who actually stood in the way of black hopes. These "liberals" spoke of their readiness for integration. Often, what they had in mind was unity on a very restricted basis. They favored a kind of one-way integration, asking black people to give up their own identity, their cultural heritage, and be swallowed up by the dominant white society. Blacks had also become weary of white "friends" who offered to fight racism anywhere—except in their own communities, where it flourished.

"We have always been a peaceful people, bearing our oppression with super-human effort," were King's earnest words, "but our memories are seared with painful experiences. . . . We hold in our hands now—broken faith and broken promises."

In Birmingham, King led an inspired black community, pledged by oath not to be violent either in words or deeds. That spring season marked a turn toward heightened direct action nationwide. By autumn, King would mount a high platform at the Lincoln Memorial in Washington, facing a quarter of a million people. They gathered to mark the hundred years that had passed since the Emancipation Proclamation had promised blacks liberty—which was still not theirs.

In words to stir the hearts of Americans of whatever race, the Reverend Martin Luther King, Jr., spoke in eloquent anger against the bigotry that robbed his people of their rights.

"I have a dream," King cried out, the refrain coming like a strong, rolling surf.

> I have a dream that my four little children will one day live in a nation where they will not be judged by the color of their skin but by the content of their character.
>
> I have a dream that one day this nation will rise up, live out the true meaning of its creed: We hold these truths to be self-evident, that all men are created equal.

Rarely can twenty-five million people agree on a single leader or on a common course of action. And black Americans in the 1960s responded to a wide range of appeals, expressing a variety of approaches to their own liberation. Some organizations had been at work for half a century. Scores of new movements appeared, led by younger men and women, many of them brilliant and capable.

The 1960s saw black Americans strike out vigorously for their own freedom. They affirmed with pride their own identity as a people. Some found enrichment in delving into their African past. Others explored black life in America as a distinct culture, with its own styles of life, standards of beauty, goals for the future.

They gloried in the victories of dark-skinned people the

world over who were fighting to throw off the white imperialist powers that had ridden their backs and robbed their wealth for hundreds of years. Black people in America recognized that they had no time to wait in a country that called itself the sweet land of liberty.

Millions responded to the cry of "Black Power," a slogan with many meanings. Some were ready to use every militant means to gain freedom. To others, Black Power represented a self-help effort to unite the black people in order to bargain for their needs from a position of strength. They meant to use their buying power in order to secure jobs. Ten million black voters were an important political balance of power. Many emphasized community control in the black districts—of schools and jobs, of business and politics. Still others saw a people more numerous than any African nation except Nigeria—black America twenty-five million strong, but still woefully powerless.

More than an organized movement, Black Power was a mood of growing self-confidence and unity. This was a people no longer willing to be judged and led by the white man. Their cause was their own. An effective black leader was expected to be hated and feared by the white world; it was a sign of his trustworthiness.

In this time of growing tension, the enemies of liberty were not idle. Countless attempts sought to divide the freedom crusade, to weaken and destroy it. Endlessly, moves were made to discredit the organizations of the black people, to break their spirit and impose on them the will of white power. At last came an effort aimed at depriving the liberation movement of its leadership. One by one, black leaders were imprisoned, exiled, killed.

Medgar Evers, the outstanding Mississippi freedom fighter, was ambushed and slain at his doorstep in the

summer of 1963. The militant and dynamic Malcolm X
was killed in 1965. In 1968, a rifle bullet ended the life of
the Reverend Martin Luther King, Jr.

Fury and grief surged through every black community
in the nation. The freedom fight had only begun to win
its first small victories—and so pitifully short of black
hopes. Yet it seemed that white supremacy begrudged an
oppressed people even the dream of freedom.

In this agonized hour, black people poured out their
tears and clung to their crushed hopes. Some struck out
blindly in their rage and frustration. Senseless murder had
stirred a rash response. The ghettos across America resounded with the blast of bombs, the crash of plate-glass
windows, the cry of fire sirens in the night.

Groping for Truth

"What happened?

"Why did it happen?

"What can be done to prevent it from happening again?"

The questions were those of President Lyndon B. Johnson. They lay like a bewildering riddle before the eleven
men and women whom the President had chosen to find
the answers.

In a series of "long, hot summers," urban America had
turned fiery and ominous. A hundred black ghettos exploded. Frustration and outrage, which had long been
mounting up, blasted into fury and flame. Sweltering days
gave way to blazing nights. Cincinnati, Ohio, and Plain-
field, New Jersey; Detroit, Michigan, and Tampa, Florida
—the outbreaks were random and unpredictable.

It seemed that the tiniest spark could touch off a new
blowup. And where next? Suddenly, this was a nation

caught in a firetrap of its own making. Even the White House betrayed the widespread feeling of fear, panic, and helplessness.

In an effort to do something, anything, the President set up a National Advisory Commission. The eleven members of the Commission seemed to have been chosen mainly for their moderate views, men and women unlikely to do or say anything very new or startling. The group was headed by Otto Kerner, the Democratic governor of Illinois, with John V. Lindsay, Republican mayor of New York City as vice-chairman. The rest of the so-called Kerner Commission was a middling model of balance—four congressmen representing both political parties, two from each house of Congress; a labor leader and an industrialist; the director of the NAACP and the police chief of Atlanta, Georgia. The eleventh member was a Kentucky woman, a state official.

The very meeting room of the Commission in Washington seemed unpromising. Its walls whispered of official United States racism, of betrayal through countless broken pledges. "The Eleven" convened in the old State Department building—in the Indian Treaty Room.

Were these people likely to get to the core of the problem? Or was this to be just one more government probe, ending with a report that hid more than it revealed? Few people were prepared for the surprise which was to come.

In the months that followed, the Commission members visited fire-gutted communities strewn with rubble, poked among charred ruins, sifted the grim facts, talked to countless witnesses and victims. In amazement, they learned that the initial incidents which led to appalling death and destruction were often trivial. A group of overheated children had illegally turned on a fire hydrant. White policemen had raided a noisy tavern in a black neighborhood. A rumor of violence had set off real violence. A wild pistol shot in the dark had brought volleys of National Guard rifle fire. A white storekeeper had overcharged a black customer and started an argument.

The Commission was forced to conclude that the disorders were not part of "any organized plan or 'conspiracy.'" There were countless illegal acts, such as the looting of stores and fire bombings, which needed to be dealt with by the courts. But these outbreaks were not merely waves of lawlessness. The Commission found that the situation could not be analyzed strictly in conventional terms of crime and punishment. Something else was clearly at work here. Summoning its courage and honesty, The Eleven confronted the problem head-on. Without blinking, they set down the cause of the disorders in clear, bold language,

"White racism is responsible."

While they condemned the use of violence, the Commission made it clear that black people fighting for their freedom were actually serving the nation. "Negro protest, for the most part," stated the Kerner report, "has been firmly rooted in the basic values of American society, seeking not their destruction but their fulfillment."

The Eleven probed deeper and deeper into their task. They found the sources of today's disorder running through the entire history of America. More than a hundred years after slavery, the nation was still haunted by that abominable institution. The poverty of black people was grounded in the unpaid labor of slavery days and in the poorly paid labor of today. The present-day sufferings of the ghetto were rooted in old doctrines of the master race which had long outlived slavery.

"Race prejudice has shaped our history decisively," the Commission declared. "It now threatens to affect our future." Prejudice was not only in the minds of individuals.

It had soaked into the major institutions of this nation, including the government itself.

Discrimination based on race was something entirely distinct from that suffered by white groups. Yes, poor European immigrants overcame prejudice and "made it" in America—but that was because they were white and were eventually accepted into the dominant white society. In spite of prejudice, the Kerner report pointed out, the white immigrant always had the promise of "the American dream."

"For the Negro family in the urban ghetto there is a different vision—the future seems to lead only to a dead end."

Members of the Commission had never before known the ghetto as a first-hand experience. Dazed and shaken by the poverty they found there, they reported: "What white Americans have never fully understood—but what the Negro can never forget—is that white society is deeply implicated in the ghetto. White institutions created it, white institutions maintain it, and white society condones it."

After years of active struggle for civil rights, there had been some talk of progress. But racism was still the overriding evil of this land. The ghetto was still intact. In fact, the Commission offered evidence that American society was moving toward even greater segregation, with whites streaming out toward all-white suburbs and blacks concentrated in the central cities. Upper and middle class suburbs were not places with no Negro problem; they had become symbols of America's white problem, strongholds of Jim Crow.

Although the wages of some blacks were somewhat higher, white income had advanced much more—so that the economic gap was wider than ever. More than half of all the poor children in the central cities were black, the Commission discovered.

The Kerner report made it clear that blacks were the victims of the doctrine of white supremacy—

> the persistent, pervasive racism that kept them in inferior segregated schools, restricted them to ghettos, barred them from fair employment, provided double standards in courts of justice, inflicted bodily harm on their children, and blighted their lives with a sense of hopelessness and despair.

Nevertheless, the Commission held out a fighting chance for change. The most urgent part of their message called for action on employment, education, welfare, and housing. They demanded not only funds for these programs but also the inclusion of blacks in the decision making, the sharing of authority and power.

"The primary goal must be a single society," stated the Kerner report, "in which every citizen will be free to live and work according to his capabilities and desires, not his color."

The Commission was itself a hopeful sign of change. From this "moderate" group came a penetrating self-examination of America's deep inner conflict. Their report seemed to suggest that any fair-thinking, open-minded group of citizens might reach similar constructive answers, once they had a willingness to find them. Clearly, their experiences had been sobering, and even painful at times. Commission members squarely confronted their own prejudice and overcame it. They suggested just such a course for all of white America.

A truly free, democratic society could not be achieved in any other way. The problem that gripped the nation could not be overcome, said the Kerner Commission, "until the fact of white racism is admitted."

THE SEVENTIES AND AFTER
Are You Part of the Problem?

The United States has long been a riddle in black and white. Even the most hard-bitten segregationists have never claimed to know exactly where one race ends and the other begins.

One of the most famous men in American legal history was Homer Adolph Plessy, the central figure in the Supreme Court case *Plessy* v. *Ferguson*. In 1896 the high court forbade him the use of "white" railroad coaches. His parents and grandparents and seven of his eight great-grandparents were all white. But Plessy was considered to be a Negro.

Recently, Chinese-American public-school children in Boston were officially declared "white." A week later the ruling was reversed, so that they were classified "non-white." Similar vague terms are used frequently by government and social agencies—as though there were two races, "white" and "other races."

What is a race, and who are the members of it? In answering these questions, great confusion has been shown by the United States government, and particularly by the agency periodically charged with classifying each man, woman, and child. Every ten years the Bureau of Census has changed the rules.

For years the census takers, in recording the race of United States residents have been told, "When in doubt, judge for yourself." In 1960 the Bureau of the Census instructed its employees to "classify as Negro any descendant of a black man, unless the Negro is regarded as an Indian in the community."

The 1970 census showed some improvements, but much

bewilderment, nonetheless. A Moor was classified as "Negro or black"—except in Delaware or New Jersey, where he was listed as "Other." A Turk was "White," except in South Carolina; there he was "Other." The government interviewers were told to tally as "White" those who answered the question on race with such replies as "Homo Sapiens, Pink, Polka Dot, Purple, Human, Spotted, Vanilla, etc."

In recent years the trend in census-taking has been to rely on the answers given by the people interviewed. The practice has somewhat changed the social meaning of "race." Actually, the word has more than one meaning. In addition to the biological *facts* about race, there are also the *ideas* of race in the minds of people.

Most dangerous of all have been the attempts to fix legal definitions of race. In the past, such laws in America and abroad have restricted the rights of certain people. "Racial" laws were used against a minority group—in the case of the Jews of Nazi Germany—and against a majority—in the Union of South Africa, whose blacks are the victims of apartheid. Similar laws were once on the statute books of many of the states in the United States.

Race came to be regarded as very important in America from the moment when men could legally be held in servitude for life because of their color. By law, slavery has been abolished. But in the lives of a great many American families, race still has an urgent, personal significance. It often makes the difference between poverty and comfort, between opportunity and hopelessness—even between life and death. The word "race" will continue to have an important social meaning as long as racism exists.

There is no scientific way of ascertaining the race of any individual. Thus it now seems to make more sense to deal with an individual's race as a social description, which one largely decides for one's self.

The 1970 census clearly showed that in some parts of the United States people have increasingly identified themselves as American Indians.

Americans of Mexican ancestry tend to see themselves as a distinct people and many prefer to be called Chicanos. They do not constitute a biologically defined race. However, many describe themselves as part of *la raza,* a term which literally means "the race" but has much broader implications. They have long been treated by white people as an inferior race, and this has helped to give them a strong sense of common identity.

As for dark-skinned people of African descent, recent years have seen a surge of strong self-identification not only with blackness as a racial description, but also with the entire range of black history and culture.

A large number of black people now reject the term "Negro." Supposedly referring to people of African origin, the word is not from any African language. It is derived from European sources, a term chosen by the whites who brought blacks here as slaves.

Out of the black experience in this land has come a distinct and proud heritage. Blacks have scored significant achievements in every field where they were permitted to do so. If they have excelled in some pursuits and not in others, this is a matter of social conditions and not biology. There are no genes for jazz—although this type of music has emerged from the black community as one distinguished contribution of America to the arts of the world.

The black man in this country is recovering his long-lost or long-concealed cultural endowment. Although now firmly rooted in American soil, he looks back to forebears who created in Africa complex societies and high civilizations, and contributed richly to the arts and sciences of all mankind.

In this nation the blacks have a proud tradition of being ever on the side of democracy and progress. Their efforts as a people were unswervingly in behalf·of the American dream. In the light of this country's highest ideals and goals, black people have mounted up a heroic and enviable record in the service of human freedom. Black history and black heroes are part of the priceless heritage of America.

In spite of severe problems, black people have achieved certain life styles in which they take an earnest pride. Even under inhuman ghetto conditions, they have found a richly human identity. These are communities in which men call each other "Brother." Something distinctive has been created out of striving and defeat, struggle and hope.

Vexed by the brutality of racism, some blacks live with a constant sense of their own anger. Some have rejected everything "white." Others stress the creative and positive struggle for control of their own lives, for the power to cast off the burdens of racist oppression. Black America has largely rejected the white man's standards, models, values.

As a social and racial grouping, still unfree, blacks voice a common yearning for liberty. Beyond that, they differ as widely as do the individuals of all other groups. Skin color does not denote personality. Nor do racial similarities ever limit the immense range of individual differences.

People and Pigeonholes

A scientist once described "every man" in these riddle-like terms: In some respects, he is like *all* other men, like *some* other men, like *no* other man.

In an effort to cope with bewildering human diversity and complexity, attempts have been made to put men into neat slots. Human beings have been sorted out by nationality, personal wealth, blood type, religious preference, occupation, size, and shape. Most troublesome of all has been the effort to classify mankind by race.

The problem is not merely that the idea of race seems to bring on strong emotional responses. Nor does the trouble lie only with the long-time confusion between the science of race and the nonscience—or nonsense—of race.

Even the best modern scientific understanding of racial variations contains large areas of the unknown. By its very nature, race is a matter of shadowy distinctions, ever changing, arising from the mists of mankind's distant past.

If human races first appeared under conditions of isolation, it may be foreseen that racial differences may someday disappear as mankind becomes increasingly a single but highly diverse population. However, this far-distant prospect can hardly become the "solution" to today's urgent problems of race relations.

No two persons are alike. And no free and open society survives without taking into account its own inner diversity. The hope for mankind seems to lie in a healthy attitude toward cultural and racial differences. A modern view of race stresses not "color-blindness" but acceptance and trust and respect toward peoples of other colors and other customs. Further, the wholesome recognition of racial differences is based on the way people want to be identified and not on any ulterior motives toward others.

Slavery in the United States was a two-race relationship. It consisted of the owners and the owned. The difference was related to skin color. For those who controlled the system, the concept of fixed, unchanging racial lines was necessary, and rigidly maintained. But such divisions were not based on science or truth or humanity.

Today the scientist knows that it is not possible to assign every individual in the world to a race, based on appearance. Skin color comes in continuous variation so that there is no line of separation. Some "white" people are darker than some black people. While some individuals may seem to fall into clear-cut racial types, a great many persons are visibly "borderline," carrying genes which came down to them from ancestors of mixed racial stocks.

Generally, scientists agree on such broad, overlapping categories as the Mongoloid, Negroid, and Caucasoid racial groupings. But there is no unity whatever among scientists on the number of races that exist in the world or the numbers of people that comprise each of them—nor is such agreement likely. Inherited differences between peoples are a matter of slight degree—but there is no device for measuring the degrees!

As a result, some scientists see only three races while others list three hundred. Most estimates are somewhere between, the common numbers being five, six, nine, thirty. There is an important group of anthropologists who have abandoned the term "race" altogether. They see it as "a dangerous four-letter word," more troublesome than useful. One leading biologist states that most of the world's people are so racially indistinct that they are members of "no race."

And yet, race is an important concept to the biologist. It has a precise scientific meaning, along with such terms as breed, strain, subspecies. From Darwin's time to the present, biologists have probed into the processes by which differentiated forms of life occur. Among plants and animals, such varieties may appear either by chance in the wild or through the controlling efforts of man. Even though the racial differentiation of mankind occurred hundreds of thousands of years ago, human races are still interesting to the scientist studying genetics.

Inheritance of traits is similar in man and in lower animals. And some of the clearest insights about mankind have come from those who have spent most of their lives studying the tiny fruit fly known as *Drosophila*. One of the American scientists is Theodosius Grigorievich Dobzhansky.

This Russian-born biologist has been a specialist in the genetics of the fruit fly, avidly pursuing its many hereditary variations in his own laboratory and in the far reaches of the world. However, the most urgent concern of Dobzhansky is mankind. And this gentle, blue-eyed professor with wisps of graying hair, has probed the deepest mysteries of mankind's races.

For Dobzhansky, the fruit fly offered a simplified, speeded-up view of genetic processes. Living through fourteen generations in a single year and passing on to its offspring a very small number of easily identifiable genes, *Drosophila* provided a revealing model of how races form and of what they consist.

Out of such research came the view that races are best studied not as types of individuals but as changing populations. In a given species, the total of all the genes present in all the individuals may be considered as a bank from which genes will be drawn by all future offspring. Most of the genes are typical of the entire species. But in an isolated population, a few genes may be distinctive—so that they identify a race within the species.

In reality, genes are not traits in themselves. They carry information or instructions through their chemistry, determining how an organism develops in its environment. A gene bank has been compared to the storage unit of a computer. As units of heredity, the genes are distributed to the offspring like the familiar computer punchcards which contain information. A grouping of individuals who draw from a restricted gene bank may constitute a race.

In human populations, isolated, restricted gene banks may have existed in the time of man's early days on earth. However, modern populations draw increasingly from a single, common gene bank. Nevertheless, there are still groupings of people who tend toward a greater or lesser sharing of those genes which produce a few distinctive physical traits that form the basis for modern races.

Scientists have emphasized that all mankind takes part in the common genetic heritage which gives fundamental unity to the human physical form. Although varied, human beings are of one species. And proof of that lies in the fact that man everywhere is a single, interbreeding population. Race is no biological barrier in the exchanging of genes.

It was Dobzhansky who brought into the 1970s a clear definition of race from the biologist's viewpoint. "Races can be defined," he said, "as populations that differ in the frequencies or in the prevalence of certain genes."

His view of races is that they are fluid and flexible. Although seen as a biological unit, each race is in the process of continuous change from the moment of its origin. In their emphasis on the genetic basis of races, Dobzhansky and other scientists have clearly excluded any and all traits which stem from acquired, learned, or cultural sources. These have nothing to do with race. "Genes create the setting for cultural traits," Dobzhansky pointed out, "but they do not compel the development of any particular ones."

Often such acquired characteristics as languages, behavior patterns, religious beliefs, occupational preferences have been falsely seen as racial. However, the biologists have stressed that race accounts only for a few slight physical differences. Most of these are superficial—"from the skin out."

The genes involving skin color affect the quantity of skin-darkening melanin, a substance present in all human beings except those rare individuals of all races who are albinos. Inherited racial differences appear in patterns of fingerprints. Among Negroids and Caucasoids, the lines on the skin at the fingertips more frequently are fully rounded whorls; in most Mongoloids the lines are more like waves than loops.

"From the skin in," racial differences reveal variations in body chemistry. The wax that accumulates in the ears of Orientals and American Indians is likely to be dry and crumbly; among Africans and Europeans it is more frequently moist and sticky. Australian aborigines are less able than Africans and Asians to detect certain bitter-tasting chemical compounds.

Blood research has also shown certain differences which in limited ways correspond to racial populations. Blood type O, for example, is more common in American Indians than in any other racial group.

In recent years, numerous methods for classifying blood have been discovered in addition to the main factors A, B, and O. The highest percentage of persons lacking the blood factor Rh, a condition important in childbirth, is found in white populations. East Asians and Australian aborigines have a relatively high frequency of what is called the Duffy factor in their blood. Black people are prone to a disease known as sickle-cell anemia, in which red-blood cells have a shrunken, sickle-like shape.

Racial differences may also occur in the length and form of bones, and shapes of teeth are clues to racial ancestry.

Professor Dobzhansky has stressed the fact that while no two groups of people are alike, "superior and inferior has no meaning."

"Genetic differences between races are secondary to those differences rooted in cultural heredity," the biologist pointed out, "and every human race has the ability to develop culture, to learn from experiences and to change." No race has superior genes.

Bigotry at My Lai

In the midsummer of 1971, a poll-taker in Oklahoma questioned white people on their racial attitudes. He found a startling range of views.

The widest differences of opinion were not between town and country folk, men and women, rich and poor. The sharpest disagreements were between young and old.

There is hardly an opinion poll that doesn't record the same result. The pattern is confirmed by casual, everyday events that occur in the lives of American youth. On the subject of race, there are clear and measurable differences in the attitudes of young people as compared to those of adults and the elderly. Generally, the new generations are less willing to accept bigotry and race hatred and the theory of the master race.

Many young people are today asking searching questions about some of their own country's policies and practices. They have seen their parents become hysterical and violent against integration in the schools, only to find out for themselves that racially mixed classrooms were not what they were led to believe. They have learned that the old "blood" myths of race do not stand up in the light of scientific truth. In studying America's quest for democracy and peace, they discover that the aims of white supremacy do not lead toward those goals.

There is a humanness in many young people that sees the humanness of others. If there is some hope for a solution to "the white problem" of this nation, undoubtedly it lies with the young. To some extent, young people have responded to America's crisis of human relations at its natural beginnings, by facing the crucial questions of prejudice within themselves. Many have mulled the challenging personal question: Are you part of the solution, or part of the problem?

However, recent years have also found young people in the forefront of racist violence. Their faces, contorted with hatred, have been seen in the television news accounts of white mobs attacking civil rights groups, overturning school buses bearing black children, showering rocks on black neighbors. Some members of the new generation have been swept along by the powerful forces of bigotry that play such an influential role in American life.

Much of America's wealth rests on a foundation of white supremacy. Political power in many areas is maintained by keeping black people powerless. Decision-making rests firmly in the hands of white society. Many government programs have a subtle racial bias. America's foreign policies are often directed by factors of "color." War itself generates the wildest of hatreds, often unloosed in great violence against dark-skinned peoples.

In the spring of 1971 a momentous court trial drew to its disturbing close. The case seemed to center on violations of military orders. In reality, it involved deep questions of the worth of human life, and whether skin color somehow affects the value of human beings.

First Lieutenant William L. Calley, Jr., a youthful platoon leader of American troops in Vietnam, was on trial for mass murder. "Rusty" Calley was not a very unusual person. To many Americans it was a frightening fact that Calley and those who were with him in the grisly happenings were such "average, normal American young men."

The trial revealed what took place on a muggy March morning in the Vietnamese village of My Lai. Briefly, the facts were these:

Charlie Company, 1st Battalion, 20th Infantry, was flown into the hamlet on a more or less routine mission. A thorough search of the town disclosed no trace of the enemy, no weapons. There were only unarmed civilians in a war-battered hamlet, eating their breakfast, praying in the temple, working in the rice paddies.

It was about 8:00 A.M. when a large number of villagers were rounded up in the town square. Without warning, the Americans opened fire with automatic weapons. During the next two hours, the GIs methodically killed the townsfolk, women, small children, babies in arms, and old men. By ten o'clock, some four hundred civilians were dead. The last large group was ordered into a drainage ditch. Burst after burst of rapid fire left not a single person alive. That was My Lai.

The United States military high command congratulated Charlie Company for "a job well done." The whole matter might have rested there, along with many other unpublicized atrocities on a smaller scale committed in Vietnam. However, after twenty months, a shame-ridden soldier revealed the facts back home. Unable to suppress the story, the Army ordered a court martial of Lieutenant Calley. The short, boyish-looking platoon leader was tried for "the murder of Oriental human beings." In the end, one man was convicted of a crime for which perhaps a great many others also bore responsibility.

Except for those persons and groups who tried to make a hero out of Calley, most Americans reacted in strained silence. It was as though the nation as a whole looked at the massacre, shuddered, and turned away.

My Lai? Had not America been there before, countless times? At Hamburg, South Carolina, where Ben Tillman's Red Shirts slaughtered the black townsfolk? At Rock Creek, Colorado, where Chinese workers were killed as a group? At Wounded Knee, South Dakota, where army guns scattered the bodies of Sioux Indians in the snow?

A black writer, a syndicated newspaper columnist, declared: "The Vietnamese civilians killed by Calley apparently do not qualify as humans, but—in servicemen's lingo —as 'gooks' or subhumans who can be exterminated much like animals. This American attitude toward people of color dates back to the founding of this country."

A psychiatric report on Calley described his state of mind during the terrible events at My Lai: "He did not feel as if he were killing humans, but rather that they were animals."

The Calley trial probed very carefully into the military orders which came down to the young lieutenant that morning. But what about the instructions which Calley had been getting all his life? What had his dominant white society taught him about people with dark skins and the value of their lives?

The perplexing questions from the dead village of My Lai were not as brand new as they seemed to be. They were as old as racism in America.

A Riddle Remains

To this day, this nation is an arena of racial conflict. It has been from the beginning.

This country's soil was blood-stained in strife over mythical differences in men's blood. Its plains rattled with the superior firepower of a "superior" race. Its cities became battlegrounds, showing ugly scars of race hatred. In a land of great wealth, a large mass of dark-skinned people were bound to lives so wretched that they had nothing to lose.

The struggle over "race" is daily news, as new as it is old. The clash of "color" has never died down since it began. Men are yet driven to dominance and violence out of strong beliefs in their own racial supremacy.

Racism in the United States did not perish with the end of slavery or with the discoveries of modern science on race. It lives. Still implanted deeply in white America is the teaching that all skin colors except white represent an inferior form of life. America seems unwilling to give up that notion—and unable to live with it, in peace.

However, lack of information may no longer serve as an excuse for bigotry. In this century, the truth about race became available to every man and woman willing to listen to reason. As scientific knowledge about race began to piece itself together, the United States acquired the opportunity to become a truly free and united nation. Slowly, research began to confirm that all men were certainly all one species. There was only one mankind, with racial differences far less important than human similarities.

The white race was as good as any other but superior to none. And if this came as a shock to the arrogance of some white people, it was knowledge they could learn to accept. In previous ages, men also came to understand painful truths through scientific discovery, and to benefit by them.

In the fifteenth century men had believed smugly that they and their planet had been favored with a place at the very center of the universe. But Copernicus disturbed their comfort with the idea that the earth was only one of several planets harnessed to the sun.

Until the eighteenth century, men enjoyed the notion that they were the lords of creation, superbeings in God's own image, chosen to dominate the earth. Darwin revealed that man evolved from the same humble origins as did the mackerel and the morning glory.

Man shook off the stubborn idea of a flat earth—and suddenly found himself free to explore the planet. He overcame the dogma of the divine right of kings, making democratic societies possible. By giving up his ancient superstitions about disease, man was then able to curb the great plagues and prolong his life span.

Modern science has upset the myth that one race is biologically superior to another. If they should ever accept the truth in full, white people might find they have shed a crushing burden.

Many riddles of race still remain. Probably the most puzzling of them all is this: if the truth about race is known at last, why does racism still survive?

Notes on Sources

Full details of the sources designated here only by the author's last name are given in the list of "Suggestions for Further Reading" on pp. 215–16.

Page	THE PROBLEM

13   For Jefferson's original wording in the Declaration of Independence on the subject of slavery, see Carl L. Becker, *The Declaration of Independence* (Knopf, 1960), pp. 212–13.

13   Jefferson's "suspicion" about races is in his book *Notes on the State of Virginia* (University of North Carolina Press, 1955).

14   Many modern historians now agree that up until the twentieth century it was a rare event to find a white American who did not believe fully in white supremacy. In *Race and Politics* (Lippincott, 1969), Prof. James A. Rawley states: "Belief in Negro inferiority was all but universal."

15   See Winthrop D. Jordan, *White Over Black* (University of North Carolina Press, 1968) for Jefferson's stand on slavery, pp. 429–81; the interchange with Banneker, pp. 449–57. Jefferson's "firebell" remark is in his letter to John Holmes, April 22, 1820.

17   The entire story of the Covey-Douglass fight is told in Douglass's own words in Frederick Douglass, *My Bondage and My Freedom* (Arno Press and The New York Times, 1969).

21   America's expanding democracy, "for whites only," is described in Arthur M. Schlesinger, Jr., *The Age of Jackson* (Little, Brown, 1945).

21   The limited rights of bondsmen as well as laws forbidding the education of slaves are reported in Stanley M. Elkins, *Slavery* (University of Chicago Press, 1959), pp. 59–60. See also Michael Banton, *Race Relations* (Tavistock, 1967), pp. 120–22.

21   For conditions among free Negroes see Leon F. Litwack, *North of Slavery* (University of Chicago Press, 1961).

Page

22   The profitability of slavery is discussed by Kenneth N. Stampp, *The Peculiar Institution* (Knopf, 1965); see ch. 9, "Profit and Loss." This book also recounts slave resistance to the plantation system, pp. 97–109. Also see Richard Hildreth, *Despotism in America* (Whipple and Damrell, 1840).

24   The use by slaveholders of the biblical story of "God's curse on Ham" is detailed in Jordan, *op. cit.*, pp. 17–20, 35–37, and 54–56.

THE EIGHTEEN FIFTIES

25   William Stanton, in *The Leopard's Spots* (University of Chicago Press, 1960), describes Morton and the other scientists who developed the polygenist theory of race. Morton's major work is *Crania Americana*, published in Philadelphia, 1839. For Nott's views, see Louis L. Snyder, *The Idea of Racialism* (Van Nostrand, 1962), p. 69. Also Gossett, pp. 64–67 and 74–77; and Handlin, pp. 64–71.

28   In *The Invention of the Negro* (P. S. Eriksson, 1966), Earl Conrad summarizes nineteenth-century thought: "The pseudo-science of race, off to a start in the time of Jefferson, was by the 1850s a thriving, circulating, powerfully mind-influencing phenomenon."

29   For Agassiz's views, see Edward Lurie, *Louis Agassiz, A Life in Science* (University of Chicago Press, 1960), particularly ch. 7, "Agassiz, Darwin and Transmutation."

30   The dating of the Creation is discussed by Banton, *op. cit.*

32   The *Richmond Enquirer* quoted is dated July 6, 1854.

32   Douglass's speech, "The Claims of the Negro Ethnologically Considered," was delivered at Western Reserve College, July 12, 1854, and is printed in full in Philip Foner, *The Life and Writings of Frederick Douglass* (International Press, 1950), vol. 2, beginning p. 292.

35   On Douglass's attitude toward the white abolitionists, see "The Anti-Slavery Movement," a lecture before the Rochester, N.Y., Ladies Anti-Slavery Society, reprinted in

Page

Foner, *op. cit.*, vol. 2. Also see "Frederick Douglass, Father of the Protest Movement," in Lerone Bennett, Jr., *Pioneers of Protest* (Johnson, 1968). For attitudes of white abolitionists on race, see Leon F. Litwack, Rochester, N.Y., *op. cit.*, ch. 7, "Abolitionism: White and Black."

37   See S. I. Kutler, editor, *The Dred Scott Decision* (Houghton-Mifflin, 1967), and Vincent C. Hopkins, *Dred Scott's Case* (Atheneum, 1967).

38   The Lincoln-Douglas debates appear in Roy Basler, ed., *Abraham Lincoln, Collected Works*, vol. 3 (Rutgers University Press, 1953). The Charleston debate is described in Carl Sandburg, *Abe Lincoln, The Prairie Years* (Harcourt, Brace, 1926), pp. 144–46.

THE CIVIL WAR YEARS

43   Gray's views on race and on Agassiz's and Darwin's theories are contained in A. Hunter Dupree, *Asa Gray* (Harvard University Press, 1959).

47   For an account of the nineteenth-century discoveries of the fossils of early man, see Dobzhansky.

48   Lincoln's dilemma is reviewed in Eli Ginzberg and Alfred S. Eichner, *The Troublesome Presence*, ch. 5, "The Agony of Lincoln" (The Free Press of Glencoe, 1964).

49   Stephens's speech was delivered at the Savannah, Ga., Atheneum, March 21, 1861. The resolution of Congress on slavery appears in *Cong. Globe* 37, July 1861.

49   Douglass's comments on Lincoln's leadership are in Foner, *op. cit.*, vol. 3, p. 116. In a later speech in Foner, *op. cit.*, vol. 4, p. 312, in tribute to the deceased Lincoln, whom he had supported strongly, Douglass declared: "He [Lincoln] was preeminently a white man's President, entirely devoted to the welfare of white men. He was ready and willing at any time during the first years of his administration to deny, postpone, and sacrifice the rights of humanity in the colored people to promote the welfare of the white people of this country. . . . He came into the

Page

> Presidential chair upon one principle alone, namely opposition to the extension of slavery. His arguments in furtherance of this policy had their motive and mainspring in his patriotic devotion to the interests of his own race."

50   For Lincoln's speech on colonization to the Committee of Negroes, see Basler, *op. cit.*, vol. 5, p. 372. For Negro reaction, see Benjamin Quarles, *Lincoln and the Negro* (Oxford, 1962), pp. 117–18.

52   On Negro troops in the Civil War, see Carter G. Woodson and C. H. Wesley, eds., *The Negro in Our History* (Associated Publishers, 1966).

54   On the Ku Klux Klan, see Allen W. Trelease, *White Terror* (Harper and Row, 1971).

DECADE OF DECISION

55   General Sheridan's oft-quoted remark was a comment he made at Fort Cobb, Indian Territory, January 1869.

55   For scalp bounties, check Gossett, p. 229, and Farb, pp. 122–24. See also O. B. Faulk, *Arizona, A Short History* (University of Oklahoma Press, 1970).

56   On broken Indian treaties, including the 1868 Treaty of Fort Laramie on the Black Hills, see Vine De Loria, Jr., ed., *Of Utmost Good Faith* (Straight Arrow Books, 1971).

57   Commissioner Walker's statement appeared in his *Annual Report*, 1872. The Topeka newspaper is quoted in Farb, p. 255.

58   Morgan's story is told in Carl Resek, *Lewis Henry Morgan, American Scholar* (University of Chicago Press, 1960); and H. R. Hays, *From Ape to Angel* (Knopf, 1958), chs. 2 and 5. See also Lewis Henry Morgan, *League of the Ho-De-No-Sau-Nee or Iroquois* (Dodd, Mead, 1922).

62   The post–Civil-War campaigns against the Indians are summarized in Farb, pp. 131–32, 225–59.

63   The Colorado congressman quoted was Rep. James B. Belford in *Cong. Record*, 46th Cong. 2nd Session, p. 4262.

63   See James Monaghan, *Life of General George Armstrong Custer* (Little, Brown, 1959).

Page

65   The Hamburg massacre was reported on the floor of Congress by Negro Rep. Robert Smalls of South Carolina. His account is in Herbert Aptheker, ed., *The Negro People in the United States* (Citadel, 1951), pp. 610–14.

67   For a summary of Reconstruction and the Hayes-Tilden Compromise, see C. Vann Woodward, *Reunion and Reaction* (Doubleday Anchor, 1956); Robert Cruden, *The Negro in Reconstruction* (Prentice-Hall, 1969); Edward F. Frazier, *The Negro in the United States* (Macmillan, 1957); John H. Franklin, *From Slavery to Freedom* (Knopf, 1961).

67   On Tillman, see Hodding Carter, *The Angry Scar* (Doubleday, 1959), pp. 382–83.

THE EIGHTEEN EIGHTIES

67   Tillman's rise to political power is documented in George Brown Tindall's *South Carolina Negroes 1877–1900* (Louisiana State University Press, 1966).

70   See Frazier, *op. cit.*, and Gossett on Jim Crow and anti-Negro violence. See also Pierre Van der Berghe, *Race and Racism* (Wiley, 1967).

71   For the factual record of lynchings, see Allen D. Grimshaw, ed., *Racial Violence in the United States* (Aldine, 1969), pp. 56–59; also National Association for the Advancement of Colored People, *Thirty Years of Lynching in the U. S.* (Arno Press, 1969). See also Aptheker, *op. cit.*, pp. 792–806.

72   For theories of early man, see Thomas K. Penniman, *A Hundred Years of Anthropology* (G. Duckworth, 1965), ch. 4. Social Darwinism is explained in Dobzhansky, pp. 11–12; and Gossett, p. 311 ff. The main source is Richard Hofstadter, *Social Darwinism in American Thought* (Braziller, 1959).

75   Treatment of the Chinese immigrants is covered in Roger Daniels and Harry H. L. Kitano, *American Racism* (Prentice-Hall, 1970), pp. 35–45; Melvin Steinfield, *Cracks in the Melting Pot* (Glencoe Press, 1970); Carey McWilliams, *Brothers Under the Skin* (Little, Brown, 1943), pp. 87–96.

Page   TEN JINGO YEARS

78   The Dawes Allotment Act is outlined in Elaine Goodale Eastman, *Pratt, the Red Man's Moses* (University of Oklahoma Press, 1935); McWilliams, *op. cit.*; Cahn, ch. 3, "Indian Land—A Dwindling Asset." For an explanation of the Ghost Dance, see Farb, pp. 280–84.

80   The Wounded Knee Massacre is described in John Tebbel, and Keith Jennison, *The American Indian Wars* (Harper, 1960), pp. 296–97; see also *Wounded Knee Massacre Hearings* before the House Committee on Interior and Insular Affairs, 7th Cong., 2nd Sess. U. S. Government Printing Office, 1938.

82   The disfranchisement of Negroes by the use of poll tax, "grandfather clause," white primary, literacy tests is described in Ginzberg and Eichner, *op. cit.*, pp. 226–30.

82   Claude H. Nolen, *The Negro's Image in the South* (University of Kentucky Press, 1967) records that in 1900 South Carolina's "expenditure for each white pupil was $5.75 for every dollar spent in educating the Negro child; by 1915 the ratio had increased to 12 to 1."

83   For the opinions in the case of *Plessy* v. *Ferguson*, see U. S. Supreme Court 163, 1896, p. 537 ff.

83   The poem "Foreign Children" by Robert Louis Stevenson was originally published in 1883.

84   The racist aspect of American expansionism is described in Albert K. Weinberg, *Manifest Destiny* (Johns Hopkins Press, 1963) and in Woodward, pp. 72–74.

85   Douglass's speech, entitled "The Present and the Future of the Colored Race in America," given in June 1863, appears in Howard Brotz, ed., *Negro Social and Political Thought* (Basic Books, 1966), p. 267 ff.

87   For sources of the quotations from White, McKinley, Lodge, see *Emporia Gazette*, March 20, 1899; *Speeches and Addresses of William McKinley* (Doubleday and McClure, 1900); *Cong. Record*, 56th Cong., 1st Sess. p. 2627 ff.; and *Official Proceedings, Twelfth Republican National Convention*, 1900 (Philadelphia), p. 88.

89   On empire building, see Julius W. Pratt, *America's Colonial Experiment* (Prentice-Hall, 1950).

Page   THE NEW CENTURY

90   The speech by Senator Beveridge may be found in *Cong. Record,* 56th Cong., 1st. Sess. p. 708 ff.

90   " 'Race' and 'Blood,' " ch. 13, in Ashley Montagu, *Man's Most Dangerous Myth* (Harper, 1952), covers that topic. Blood types are discussed in Phillip Mason, *Common Sense About Race* (Gollancz, 1961), and Stanley M. Garn, *Human Races* (C. C. Thomas, 1961).

93   See Dobzhansky on Mendelian principles.

95   Sumner is best studied in his own writings: Albert G. Keller, ed., *Essays of William Graham Sumner,* 2 vols. (Yale University Press, 1934).

98   Du Bois tells his own story in the *Autobiography of W. E. B. Du Bois* (International Press, 1968). See also by W. E. B. Du Bois: *The Souls of Black Folk* (Fawcett, 1964) and *Dusk of Dawn* (Harcourt Brace, 1940).

98   Grimshaw, *op. cit.,* contains a vivid description of the Atlanta massacre of 1906, pp. 44–46. For details on Negro living conditions, education, and convict labor in the South at the turn of the century see Nolen, *op. cit.*

101   The visit of Boas to Atlanta is related in Melville J. Herskovitz, *Franz Boas* (Scribners, 1953), p. 111.

102   The Du Bois report on the founding convention of the NAACP is contained in Aptheker, *op. cit.,* pp. 924–27.

TIME OF TRIAL

103   Boas's early years are retold in June Helm MacNeish, ed., *Pioneers of American Anthropology* (University of Washington Press, 1966); Abram Kardiner, *They Studied Man* (World, 1961); Herskovitz, *op. cit.;* A. L. Kroeber, Ruth Benedict, and others, *Franz Boas,* Menasha, Wis., American Anthropological Association, 1943. See also Franz Boas, *The Mind of Primitive Man* (Collier, 1963).

Page

106   See U. S. Immigration Commission, Government Printing Office Doc. CD36, *Dictionary of Races or Peoples*, 1911. The *Dictionary* is discussed in Handlin.

110   See Theodora Kroeber, *Ishi* (University of California Press, 1965).

111   The remarks of Theodore Roosevelt on Indians were in a speech in New York City in January 1886, and are quoted in Hermann Hagedorn, *Roosevelt in the Badlands* (Houghton-Mifflin, 1921), p. 355.

114   Gossett describes World War I intelligence tests, pp. 364–69, 376–78, and postwar race riots, pp. 370–71.

115   Brigham's later reversal of his conclusions appears in *Psychological Review*, XXXVII (1930), p. 165.

116   Senator Vardaman's statement may be found in *Cong. Record* 55, p. 60063.

THE NINETEEN TWENTIES

117   The KKK and the "nativism" of the Twenties are described in Gossett. In John Higham, *Strangers in the Land* (Rutgers University Press, 1955), see the chapter entitled "The Tribal Twenties." See also Trelease, *op. cit.*

117   On Henry Ford and anti-Semitism, see Carey McWilliams, *A Mask for Privilege* (Little, Brown, 1948), pp. 33–37. See also Jonathan Leonard, *The Tragedy of Henry Ford* (Putnam, 1932), p. 208 ff.

118   Racial and ethnic stereotypes are discussed in Handlin.

121   Madison Grant's viewpoint is expressed in his book, *The Passing of the Great Race* (Scribners, 1923). Osborn's position appears in *Natural History*, January 1926, "The Evolution of Human Races." Also see I. A. Newby, *Jim Crow's Defense* (Louisiana State University Press, 1965).

122   Boas's letter, "Lo, the Poor Nordic," is in the *New York Times*, April 13, 1924.

123   See Herskovits, *op. cit.*, for an account of the case of the Armenians and also a summary of scientific knowledge of human races in the 1920s.

Page   CRISIS YEARS

127   For anthropology's view of early man in the 1930s, see
M. F. Ashley Montagu, *Man: His First Two Million Years*
(Columbia University Press, 1939).

129   Nazi race theories are discussed in William L. Shirer,
The Rise and Fall of the Third Reich (Simon & Schuster,
1960). See R. L. Duffus, "Franz Boas vs. Hitler," in the
New York Times Book Review, February 10, 1946.

131   The statement by Hitler is from a conversation with
Herman Rauschning, quoted in Conrad, *op. cit.*

133   For human migrations and racial differentiation, see
Amram Scheinfeld, *Your Heredity and Environment*
(Lippincott, 1965); Mason, *op. cit.;* Hampton L. Carson,
Heredity and Human Life (Columbia University Press,
1963); and Dobzhansky. See also Leslie C. Dunn, *Heredity and Evolution in Human Populations* (Harvard University Press, 1959). See also A. B. Fortuyn, "The Origin
of Human Races," *Science,* 80, 1939, pp. 352–53.

136   See St. Clair Drake and Horace R. Cayton, *Black Metropolis* (Harper & Row, 1962). For anti-Negro violence
in the cities in the 1940s, see Grimshaw, *op. cit.*

ERA OF STRIFE

140   For the story of Dr. Drew, see Richard Hardwick, *Charles
Richard Drew, Pioneer in Blood Research* (Scribners,
1967). See also Albert Deutsch, "Dr. Charles Drew, Surgeon—A Study in Blood and Race," *PM Daily,* New York,
March 30, 1944.

142   The Korematsu case and the wartime detention of Japanese are described in Bradford Smith, *Americans from
Japan* (Lippincott, 1948); Bill Hosokawa, *Nisei* (Mor-
row, 1969); and Daniel I. Okimoto, *American in Disguise*
(Walker-Weatherhill, 1971).

146   The reaction of scientists and others to the A-bombing
of Japan is detailed in Alice Kimball Smith, *A Peril and
a Hope* (University of Chicago Press, 1965).

Page

147   The Lindbergh article, entitled "Aviation, Geography and Race," is in *Reader's Digest,* November 1939.

148   On Ruth Benedict, see Kardiner, *op. cit.,* and Margaret Mead, *An Anthropologist at Work* (Houghton, 1959).

150   The impounding of the Benedict-Weltfish booklet is recorded in M. F. Ashley Montagu, *Man's Most Dangerous Myth,* Appendix B.

150   See Gunnar Myrdal, *An American Dilemma* (Harper & Row, 1962).

INTO THE FIFTIES

154   For a detailed account of racist attacks on blacks seeking housing, see Grimshaw, *op. cit.*

156   A comprehensive book on the subject of prejudice is Gordon W. Allport, *The Nature of Prejudice* (Addison-Wesley, 1954).

158   See UNESCO, *Race and Science* (Columbia University Press, 1961). For information on the Genocide Convention, see publications of the Ad Hoc Committee on the Human Rights and Genocide Treaties, 25 East 78 Street, New York, N.Y. 10021.

161   See Mary Ellen Goodman, *Race Awareness in Young Children* (Collier, 1964). See also Kenneth B. Clark, *Prejudice and Your Child* (Beacon Press, 1963). The Supreme Court decision in *Brown* v. *Board of Education,* 347, U. S. 483 (1954) is given in full in Clark, along with footnotes.

165   Senator Eastland's reaction to the Brown decision is quoted in I. A. Newby, *Challenge to the Court* (Louisiana State University Press, 1967).

166   Hawaii's struggle for statehood is recounted in Gavan Daws, *Shoal of Time* (Macmillan, 1968).

THE NINETEEN SIXTIES

168   I. A. Newby's *Challenge to the Court,* details the "scientific" racism of the 1960s. For a description of the White

Page

Citizens Councils, see Hodding Carter III, *The South Strikes Back* (Doubleday, 1959). See also J. Comas, " 'Scientific' Racism Again?" in *Current Anthropology*, ii, 1961, p. 303. For the reaction of scientists, see Margaret Mead and Theodosius G. Dobzhansky, *Science and the Concept of Race* (Columbia University Press, 1968).

171   For Coon's theories, see Carleton Coon, *The Origin of Races* (Knopf, 1962). A review of scientific reaction to Coon is contained in I. A. Newby, *op. cit.* See also Dobzhansky, "Possibility that Homo Sapiens Evolved Independently Five Times Is Vanishingly Small," *Current Anthropology*, Oct. 1963, pp. 360, 364–66. Also, M. F. Ashley Montagu, ed., *The Concept of Race* (Free Press of Glencoe, 1964), ch. 9, "On Coon's *The Origin of Races.*"

174   The Arthur Jensen article appeared in *Harvard Educational Review*, Winter 1969. The response to Jensen is in W. F. Bodmer and L. L. Cavalli-Sforza, "Intelligence and Race," *Scientific American*, Oct. 1970, pp. 19–29; J. Cass, "Race and Intelligence," *Saturday Review*, May 17, 1969, pp. 67–68. See also Richard C. Lewontin, *Bulletin of the Atomic Scientists*, March 1970, pp. 2–8. See also Banesh Hoffman, *The Tyranny of Testing* (Crowell-Collier, 1962); L. Erlenmeyer-Kimling and Lissy F. Jarvik, "Genetics and Intelligence," *Science*, Dec. 13, 1963, pp. 1477–79.

178   For a biography of the Reverend Martin Luther King, Jr., see Lerone Bennett, Jr., *What Manner of Man* (Johnson, 1964). For black attitudes in the 1960s, see Arnold Adoff, editor, *Black on Black* (Macmillan, 1968). See also Louis L. Knowles and Kenneth Prewitt, eds., *Institutional Racism in America* (Prentice-Hall, 1969).

184   See *Report of the National Advisory (Kerner) Commission on Civil Disorders* (Bantam, 1968).

THE SEVENTIES AND BEYOND

187   Plessy's ancestry is discussed in Oscar Handlin, *Fire-Bell in the Night* (Little, Brown, 1964).

Page

187   Reports on Chinese-American school children in Boston appear in the *New York Times,* Oct. 20, 1966, p. 21, and Oct. 27, 1966, p. 40.

187   The census on race is discussed in Steinfield, *op. cit.* Documents quoted are U. S. Department of Commerce, Bureau of the Census, *Enumerator's Reference Manual,* 1960, and *Questionnaire Reference Book, 1970 Census.*

191   See Stanley M. Garn, *Readings on Race* (C. C. Thomas, 1968). See also T. G. Dobzhansky, *Evolution, Genetics, and Man* (Wiley, 1963) and *Genetics of the Evolutionary Process* (Columbia University Press, 1970).

196   See *Newsweek* magazine surveys of opinions on race, conducted by William Brink and Louis Harris.

197   See Arthur Everett, Kathryn Johnson, and Harry F. Rosenthal, *Calley* (Dell, 1971).

199   The comment on the Calley case is by L. F. Palmer, Jr., columnist of the *Chicago Daily News,* April 17, 1971.

199   The psychiatric report on Calley is quoted in *Time* magazine, April 12, 1971, p. 18.

Suggestions for Further Reading

Boas, Franz. *Anthropology and Modern Life.* New York: Norton, 1962.
The anthropologist who pioneered toward a modern scientific understanding of race presents a clear, popular approach to the question.

Cahn, Edgar S., ed. *Our Brother's Keeper.* Washington, D.C.: New Community Press, 1969.
In a forceful account of Indian life today, this book shows the effect of white racism on the native Americans.

Dobzhansky, Theodosius G. *Mankind Evolving.* New Haven: Yale University Press, 1962.
An outstanding scientist explains racial differences in easily understood terms as part of the development of the human species.

Editors of *Ebony* magazine. *The White Problem in America.* New York: Lancer Books, 1966.
Racism is seen from the viewpoint of a number of outstanding black Americans.

Farb, Peter. *Man's Rise to Civilization as Shown by the Indians of North America.* New York: Dutton, 1968.
This factual account of Indian history and culture corrects many of the long-standing falsehoods about America's so-called red men.

Goldsby, Richard A. *Races and Race.* New York: Macmillan, 1971.
This is an excellent, concise explanation of the biology of races, with a particularly good summary of the processes of race formation.

Gossett, Thomas F. *Race, the History of an Idea in America.* Dallas: Southern Methodist University Press, 1963.
Discrimination is traced to its roots in the theory of superior and inferior races in this well-documented history.

Handlin, Oscar. *Race and Nationality in American Life.* New York: Doubleday, 1957.
A well-known social historian skillfully describes the turmoil caused by prejudice in the United States.

McWilliams, Carey. *Brothers Under the Skin.* Boston: Little, Brown, 1943.
Written in the 1940s, this book offers a revealing view of how America has treated Negroes, Indians, Chinese, Mexicans, and Japanese.

Ritchie, Barbara. *The Riot Report.* New York: The Viking Press, 1969.
This is a condensed, well-illustrated, and very readable version of the *Report of the National Advisory (Kerner) Commission on Civil Disorders.*

Woodward, C. Vann. *The Strange Career of Jim Crow.* New York: Oxford University Press, 1966.
A noted historian offers a study of segregation and discrimination in the United States over a period of a hundred years.

Index

ABOUT THE AUTHOR

S. CARL HIRSCH is the author of many popular books on science for young people. His first book, *The Globe for the Space Age,* was winner of the Thomas Alva Edison Foundation Award for The Best Science Book for Children in 1963, an honor awarded him again in 1966 for *The Living Community: A Venture into Ecology.* Recently the Society of Midland Authors presented him with the Clara Ingram Judson Award, in recognition of the excellence of his books and his contribution to young people's understanding of today's world.

Mr. Hirsch lives with his wife in Evanston, Illinois, a suburb of Chicago, where he has for many years conducted a Sunday class at the Unitarian Church. *The Riddle of Racism* grew directly out of this experience, which Mr. Hirsch has described as follows:

"I suppose that what led me directly into the writing of this book was a trial I attended. The case was heard not in a courtroom but in a schoolroom. My Sunday class at the Evanston Unitarian Church had decided to put 'Mr. Whiteman' on trial.

"While I watched and listened, white suburban middle-class children conducted the hearing. The harsh indictment was read. Accusing witnesses were brought in. Damaging evidence was presented. The defense could offer little vindication.

"The trial went on for many weeks. In the end, White America was found guilty before a fair judge and an honest jury of peers.

"I was convinced as never before that the race problem in America was in fact the white problem and could not be escaped. White America would not only have to free its victims but face its own guilty conscience as well. I was certain too that the young people of this land would at last see justice done."